HYPNOTIC STORYTELLING

THE ANSWERS YOU WANT

Bryan J. Westra

Indirect Knowledge Limited
MURRAY, KENTUCKY

Bryan James Westra/Indirect Knowledge Limited
2317 University Station
Murray, Kentucky/42071
www.indirectknowledge.com

Book Layout ©2014 indirectknowledge.com

Ordering Information:
Quantity sales. Special discounts are available on quantity purchases by corporations, associations, and others. For details, contact the "Special Sales Department" at the address above.

Hypnotic Storytelling/ Bryan James Westra. —1st ed.
ISBN: 978-0-9899464-5-2

CONTENTS

*Dedication to All Who Seek Indirect Knowledge—and,
Jennifer, my 'Lovey'!!!*

"You are aware of everything; yet, not aware."

—THE HYPNOTIST

CHAPTER 1

INTRODUCTION

How true it is our emotions influence our behaviors. When I was about ten or eleven my mother told me a story about how my father had left to go be with his 'other' family and how he had left her penniless and broke to take care of us children.

A day earlier I had been bragging about how much of my allowance I had saved over the years. I was proud of my accomplishment; rather than spending my allowance money, as my brother and sister had, I had saved mine and now had plenty of money, whereas they had none.

When my mother cried in front of me, explaining how there was no money; even no money to buy food with, I remember going up stairs, into the attic, where I had my treasure hid. I began crying, because my mother was sad. I couldn't control my emotions, any more than I could fully understand them critically.

In my state of sadness, I brought my treasure down from the sweltering attic, and into my mother's room. My face looked as though I had been crying, but I had been careful to dry up my tears before entering her room. I didn't want to cause her sadness with my tears; as she had caused me sadness with hers—emotions are addictive.

Walking over to where she sat, seeing her still saddened, I placed the treasure in front of her, and presented it to her as a gift of love. I hoped she would smile and be happy; instead, she cried even harder.

There are some problems money cannot solve, I learned.

Let me stop right here.

The story I just told you is entirely fictional. It never happened to me. It has the makings of a hypnotic story; namely, it begins in normalcy, than normalcy is spun on its head, it also has emotionally laden language, it also has a moral lesson that is identifiable, and causes the reader to become transported into the narrative. It is not necessarily a pretty story. In fact the ending is cut off. You may be wondering what might be the ending. You might have a visual picture of the attic, the mother's room, the amount of money which was the young child's treasure, and the type of person the father might have been.

There's a lot of things left unexplained, and for good reason. By leaving the story full of holes, leaving you guessing, the story becomes more absorbing and hypnotic. You want to know the ending, and, yet, there isn't one. You might even begin to wonder what the meaning of the story is, and if it was money or love that was really to blame for the mother's sadness—or both!

Notice this story was told quickly, and didn't have to fill up the pages of this book. If I had been telling it aloud

you would have seen my body language animated, congruent with the message I wanted you to receive and relate to.
I would have acted out emotionally the emotions I wanted
you the listener to receive; that is, the sadness experienced
by the lonely mother, and the child left to bear witness to
that sadness.

Why Hypnotic Stories?

Hypnotic stories are stories that affect change in people;
namely, changes that are linked to emotions, or to certain
behaviors. They begin as normal stories, and then various
hypnotic elements are added into the stories, to help ensure the outcomes we want happen, which are the behaviors that will result from having heard and experienced
one of our hypnotic stories.

For the hypnotist a story is perhaps the perfect vehicle
used for the purpose of bringing about change. Changing
minds is arguably easier when you use stories to hint at
the direction one should lean forward and follow towards.
Stories are indirect, most often, and never have to be direct initiatives, brought before a subject. Their intention
is subtly to induce and even seduce the subject to taking a
particular action on his or her own without being directly
influenced or persuaded to do so. In this way, stories are
beautiful works of aural art that inspire people to take actions they might otherwise not take. They stir up that
emotional aspect of who we are as human beings; you
know, the side of us we're less in touch with most of the
time. People don't want to always look at their emotions,

because when they do, they tend to make decisions that aren't always logical, and not always in their best interest—for example, the story of the young man handing over his hard saved allowance monies to his desperate and emotionally distraught mother. The money could have bought him something, but instead became a gift he felt compelled to give away.

What are Hypnotic Stories?

Hypnotic stories are ones that transport us to empathy, sometimes. This fellow feeling we understand on a level of consciousness that is less direct and more indirect in nature. When we empathize with someone we commiserate with them by showing pity with our kindness and understanding. Some people call this communicating on a soul level, but call it what you will, the ability to relate with someone through a shared experience of a story is something very hypnotic indeed.

Milton Hyland Erickson, the father of indirect hypnosis, once explained that all of our experiences take place in the brain. He explained that reliving an experience from memory possessed the same quality of 'realness' as the original act of experiencing it. In this same way, a story can walk us back through time, or have us recall something that didn't actually transpire, or make us fantasize something as real that wasn't really real at all; yet, now, is real.

This is an important point to mention. You see reification of something revivified is no different than experiencing something for the first time, originally. Reanimating a memory is no different than experiencing it from the original state you first experienced it. Interestingly, you can tell a story from memory, and the emotional subtexts associated with that memory can be very effective in affecting other people emotionally. Stories are emotional devices, just as much as they convey a contextual meaning, as well as other faintly heterogeneous meanings.

Hypnotic stories are comprised of hypnotic language mechanics, as well as structured using hypnotic fragments that serve as hypnotic representations that both induce trance, while causing the mind to search for meanings that aren't explicitly stated. Such hypnotic fragments, indirectly conveyed, have a powerful hold over the subject, making it so that they come under the spell of hypnosis.

Once hypnotized the subject is somewhere else, besides where they are. Erickson referred to this state as a 'mind without a body'. This was one of his definitions of a hypnotic trance.

In the same way, when you tell a hypnotic story, you'll achieve the same state in your subjects, in which they'll feel aware of everything; yet, not aware of anything. It is a state like a daydream; one in which you zone out, find your mind wandering, being someplace other than where you are. It happens naturally, every day, and often through each day. Nearly every 90 to 120 minutes your circadian rhythms whisk you away into hypnosis, making you perform your actions on autopilot, without consciously being able to do anything. It is the same as your breathing, your heart beating, your unconscious non-aware activities, and all your other automatic autonomic actions, happening, without your conscious awareness being needed to carry forth these actions. You're in a hypnotic state.

Experientially, you achieve hypnosis, more often than you are aware, because mostly you are unaware of this state happening to you when it happens. This is the nature of hypnosis, and a hypnotic story can take you there quite effortlessly, and in a short time, almost instantly.

How to Make a Story Hypnotic?

In this book you'll learn several ways to make your stories hypnotic. One of the easiest ways to hypnotically charge a story, which will be the bedrock of how we hypnotize all of our hypnotic stories, is simply by going into the state of hypnosis first, and telling your stories from this state of hypnosis.

The deeper hypnotized you are, the deeper the hypnotic charge will be on your story. When you are hypnotized, it is quite easy to naturally let your 'other' mind hypnotize others. The state of consciousness someone is in around us seems to affect our own state of consciousness; likewise, when we're deeply hypnotized, the tendency for others around us to enter hypnosis increases exponentially.

Even when you read a book that has been written while the author has been deeply hypnotized, the words will be charged with that same state and you'll more easily slip into hypnosis, without even knowing it is happening to you, you know?

How a story is told is also a factor in how hypnotic it will be. Emotions are contagious and so are states. The more hypnotized you are, the more hypnotized others will be around you. The more hypnotized you are when you tell your story, the more hypnotized your subject will be when they hear your story. This is the law of hypnosis; namely, the more under the spell of hypnosis you are, the more under the spell of hypnosis others will become when you tell your stories hypnotically.

After achieving this ability to operate hypnotically with some slight consciousness, and a knowing of how to achieve your end result, you'll be able to use hypnosis much more effectively to achieve your ends. You must, however, practice operating hypnotically, often in fact, in order to gain a mastery over remaining in this state of mind and carrying on consciously in some slight measure. When you first begin operating hypnotically, you'll only have some small ability to operate consciously while only slightly being hypnotized. Likewise you'll only be able to hypnotize people slightly, to disorient their critical faculty slightly. The more you practice operating hypnotically, going deeper and deeper into the hypnotic state, the more deeply the hypnotic state others will experience around you.

In my opinion this is something Erickson mastered to a great degree of mastery. He could remain very hypnotized, while hypnotizing others, and be able to function to what would appear to onlookers as being in a perfectly normal state of mind consciousness. Really, I believe, he had practiced hypnosis so much so that he was able to operate just as easily while hypnotized as otherwise.

I think being a conscious hypnotist is the pursuit of this direction, which I do believe Erickson mastered astonishingly well.

The goal of this book is to teach you how to tell hypnotic stories, by examining the literature out there, but also by having you experiment, and apply what you learn to your everyday conversations. It is only through application that you truly become a master hypnotist, and master hypnotic storyteller.

What if You Apply These Lessons In Hypnotic Storytelling?

I think once you experiment some with storytelling in general, first realizing that we tell stories all the time, whether we're mindful of it or not, and that storytelling is instilled in our culture and in our humanness, you'll feel astonished to learn that hypnotic storytelling is something you already do unconsciously already, so well.

You can also borrow stories, or retell other peoples' stories, and grab hold of some really interesting stories that can be adapted to the type of change work you're doing with a hypnotherapy client, or if you are a conversational hypnotist the type of stories that will help your sales calls and help to change the persuasions of others, covertly, and indirectly.

I was standing in line at a restaurant around an hour ago, taking a break from writing, and I heard a very interesting story. The story was told by a college girl, who has a brother, she barely talks to.

She was telling three friends how she found her brother and his girlfriend alone at her parent's house a day earlier. Her brother, she said, was only 17.

When she entered the home, the brother's girlfriend came out of his room first, disheveled looking, and hair a mess. Then out came the brother, looking annoyed.

Seeing what had happened, the girl instantly put two and two together and realized that her brother and the girlfriend were making out. She didn't call him on it, but said, talking to her group of friends, "I made sure he helped me move into my dorm today. His girlfriend rode along, but she didn't say a word to me, and never even got out of my brother's truck to help me move. She's so stuck up!"

The girl's listening to this story all agreed that the girl was stuck up and advised her to tell on her brother and let the parents know about the brother and his girlfriend making out in their house. The sister agreed that this is what she was going to do, because she didn't like the brother's girlfriend, whatsoever.

So you see this is another short story. There's some interest, some conflict, even a resolution, and it literally happened in my awareness only an hour or so ago. The point is stories happen all the time. They happen so often in fact that we're most often not aware of them when they are happening.

The Recap

This book is going to teach you how to tell hypnotic stories. You'll learn various storytelling models and how to incorporate hypnotic symbols, attributes, language patterns, conventions, and much more to transform your subject and ensure compliance and a changed mind occurs.

You'll be learning how to take ordinary stories you tell and turn them into and make them powerful hypnotic stories that connect with your subject on multiple levels. You'll also be discovering why hypnotic stories are so effective in communicating hypnotically; what they specifically do to hypnotize and change minds instantly; and how you can apply them for various purposes and outcomes; and be encouraged to experiment and find new ways to practically apply hypnotic storytelling to make you a more effective persuader and person of influence.

I hope you're ready for this incredibly exciting journey into the covert, indirect, world of hypnotic storytelling. I'm excited for you. Once you learn these skills and techniques, you will never look at storytelling the same way again. Most people find that they're appreciation and value on storytelling increases dramatically after learning these lessons in hypnotic storytelling.

CHAPTER 2

HYPNOTIC HERO'S JOURNEY

The late Joseph Campbell learnt the common thread that runs through most epics and narratives. It starts with a normal setting and then abruptly is interrupted by a sudden break, and, from there, begins a journey; one that eventually circles back around to where it first begun. This basic story model is one that begins and ends with an exciting and captivating journey. For this reason, we start here.

When I was nineteen I asked my father if I might go with him over the road (he was a long-haul truck driver) to help him deliver freight. I mostly wanted to see the United States of America and many places I had not yet been. I always enjoyed traveling.

Each day I found myself awakened in a new place. It might be Minneapolis, Minnesota one morning, and Saint

Louis, Missouri the next, or Fort Myers, Florida another; it all depended on my father's schedule.

Sometimes it was cold outside—extremely cold—well below 0° Fahrenheit. Other times it was hot—very hot—well above 100° Fahrenheit. The point is it was always different, and to me always sensational.

After traveling with him for many months I grew restless, eventually. I almost became bored. I had a lot on my mind, being so young, about my future, and what I wanted out of life. I didn't know, and this concerned me. Time seemed to pass by faster and faster with the passing of each month. A year was approaching.

I took up reading.

One book I found hypnotically captivating was the Ramayana by Valmiki. This story is a Hindu epic in which the protagonist Rama is exiled from his kingdom and forced to live as a recluse for 14 years inside the forest on the outskirts of the kingdom. His wife Sita, and brother Lakshmana accompanied him. His other brother Bharat rules in his absence.

Rama's life goes on as ordinary, until his wife Sita is one unsuspecting day taken captive by the evil demon king Ravana.

Rama is forced to go south to the island of Lanka to retrieve her.

In the end he succeeds and eventually gains his kingdom back.

The story is a prime example of Campbell's 'Hero's Journey'; namely, because it encompasses all the parts, or rather most anyway, of what Campbell finds to be true in most epics and legends.

As this is the basic story it is important to begin here with the hypnotic hero's journey, in order to really understand the essence of the hypnotic story.

Why the Hypnotic Hero's Journey?

The hypnotic hero's journey is the quintessential story we think of and learn from the start of our life. Life parallels the hypnotic hero's journey, in truth. We start with an entrance into the world that is ordinary and normal to say the least. Then we experience some type of transformation, or coming of age, or something like this. Then we embark on a journey of self-discovery and self-development. We learn about our true nature. We learn about what we're capable of? We essentially learn about life experientially; to discover our own truth, and to forge our way independently. During this journey we experience trials and tribulations, and these ordeals become lessons that make us stronger and wiser. Eventually we find our way, and we make sense of the life that we've been given; learning of our destiny or dharma, and then seek to accomplish it. Upon accomplishing it, we return back to what's the past, what's familiar, and where we began, that we might come full circle with ourselves.

So you see the hypnotic hero's journey is a story we identify and empathize with as being relevant to our own way of life. There's isomorphic parallels delivered in such stories that resolve hidden problems inside ourselves that we cannot solve. Such metaphors for ourselves are powerfully hypnotic, because they touch on the very essence of what it means to be 'human'.

What is the Hypnotic Hero's Journey?

As I've hinted at, the hypnotic hero's journey is a parallel of the human experience; namely, what it's like to be a human being, living this human existence. We all have our own unique experiences we live. There are aspects of our existence that can be found in the experiences of others. The hypnotic hero's journey is an archetypal representation of the classic story that begins in normalcy, and transitions into some great adventure that's at first unpredictable, and then peaks at some height or climax that is filled with intense emotions, and then tapers off toward an outcome which eventually leads back to where the hypnotic hero journey archetype first began, i.e. normalcy. It's a cycle; a cycle of disparagements that can stop us in our tracks or motivate us to prove our self-worth and what we're capable of achieving despite the belittlements from others and what they think of us, which all add up to many life experiences.

The quite famous author Paulo Coelho; author of The Alchemist, stated how his mother and father discouraged him from becoming a writer, preferring him to become an engineer, like his father, instead. When he refused his parents even went so far as to have him committed to a mental hospital. Knowing they only wanted what was best for him, he eventually accepts entrance into law school; but, he left a year later to embark on a personal journey, which eventually led him back to his writing career. His experiences; that is, his journey of defiance, sidestepping what others decided for him, opting instead to follow his own personal journey, led him to his ultimate success—that of a famous writer.

So you see, the hypnotic hero's journey is the greatest education, it is also the uncertainty as to if we'll realize success or failure, and a leaving behind of what's expected of us, what's the known and the familiar—what's comfortable—in lieu of the alien and nameless journey that has hypnotized us into a spellbound state of fascination where we're put under a deep, deep, trance. The journey can be scary; however, it can also be enlightening, and the source of our happiness, enthrallment, strength, and the test of our faith. The journey may also have rewards; such as: love, wealth, knowledge, power, and friendships, yet, to be discovered.

According to Campbell, this structure of the hero's journey is also coined the 'Monomyth', because it is the common thread that is the blueprint of nearly every myth and epic poem throughout history.

How to Tell the Hypnotic Hero's Journey?

Now that we know what it is and why it's the essential story of all stories we can tell, you might say we know the value of the hypnotic hero's journey, and you might say we have enough information, now, to start to narrow down enough to be able to formulate our own hypnotic hero's journey's tales. In this section I'll outline for you, briefly, Campbell's Monomyth structure, which will make it easier for you to instantly deliver the Hypnotic Hero's Journey, anytime, and anywhere—hypnotically automatically!

The Call to Adventure

Remember, we start with normal, ordinary, and, perhaps boring. It's the day to day life, someone, a character in our story, i.e. the protagonist, knows and relies on in order to assume a unique identity. In my way of thinking about it I look at it usually as a collectivistic, regulated life, that the character is born into. I'm reminded of the Indian, born into a collectivistic household, where grandparents, live with parents, who live with children. Everybody looks after everybody else, and everybody has a place, a purpose, an identity that holistically defines the entire family unit.

The call to adventure is a calling away from this collective identity toward an individual identity—away from the family unit—toward the unknown that defines individuality. It's a separation, you see.

How the call to adventure spawns can be quite different, story to story. It can be rather sudden and accidental—the merest chance—or it can be planned out and brought about over time, should you want. It really is up to the hypnotic storyteller to decide how it comes about.

Creativity plays a part in the call to action. Usually it's a captivating act that happens to set the stage for the journey. The journey is the great escape, or the great expectation, or the great expectation gone wrong.

The Refusal of the Call

Not always, but sometimes, often in fact, the protagonist hesitates in accepting the call to adventure—sometimes the protagonist refuses the journey. This can happen for a number of reasons: (a) the hero/heroine is pressured by his environment to remain where it is safe, expected, and sometimes the demands of the environment create a greater persuasion than the internal yearning to break free and go in search of a personal destiny. When this happens, the main character may experience internal dissonance—wondering, "What might have been?"

At some point the discord may build-up until a breakaway is necessary, and the character yields to destiny, and acquiesces to forego what is expected of him to embrace the journey anyway. Sometimes in this light, the protagonist must make the hard choice to give up his life by way of an ultimatum in order to go aboard the journey. This can cause the listener, i.e. the hypnotic subject to become fully captivated and transported into the story.

The Supernatural Aid

Campbell's next element to the hero-journey is the introduction of a supernatural aid, that assists the hero in some way by providing him or her with council and possibly a gift that will help with passage through the first threshold, which seeks to keep the hero/heroine from crossing over to the new world where the quest officially begins.

Remembering the story of the Bhagavad Gita, an Indian spiritual volume, in which the warrior Arjun, is required to fight against his cousins in a great battle, because it is his dharma to fight, due to being born into the Kshatriya class, I observe the parallel being Lord Krishna, consoling and bringing council to Arjun, explaining to him the reasons why he must fight a fight he at first refuses to fight. I cannot think of a better story where killing is framed as a righteous act; sold to the reader as commendable and blameless, and Godly.

In this short story, a section taken from the longest epic poem ever written; namely, The Mahabharata, the supernatural aid, is actually an incarnation of God, who happens to be the charioteer of Arjun. It is a beautifully hypnotic story—I highly recommend.

We see this type of secondary character present in so many mythological and epic tales. This character may appear and reappear just in the nick-of-time to aid the character in some powerful way. This character in my mind represents metaphorically the unexplainable forces of the universe working to aid and assist someone along their personal journey. Oftentimes it is us to the character to listen and learn from this character or rebel and desist their help, which incidentally, usually, brings with such defiance, negative consequences that impact the success of the journey.

This supernatural character is often the 'voice of reason' serving to enlighten the protagonist and to help mature him/her, and to prepare him/her for the journey ahead. This character is a wise, often old, a character that is the hypnotic symbol for wisdom and good judgment. As the reader, or listener of such a type of story, we may unconsciously relate to this character as a parental figure, or a wise grandparent who always seeks to steer us clear of danger, while preparing us for the pitfalls that lie along the path of life; that we may not fall into such traps and entanglements.

The First Threshold

Having left to discover the journey, the protagonist prove his/her worthiness to crossover into the land of the unknown. This unknown land is protected by a guardian. This guardian archetype is the first test by which the hero/heroine must prove his/her worth in order to proceed with the carrying out of the journey.

The 'unknown' which is protected by this guardian is hypnotically symbolic of the 'other mind' or the 'unconscious mind'; and the guardian archetype is hypnotically symbolic of the 'critical faculty' which acts as a filter that lets in some sensory information, while disallowing other sensory information from entering the 'mind'.

From a hypnotic storytelling perspective these hypnotic symbols are important to understand, because they are metaphors representing the hypnotic process which naturally occurs when a hypnotic storyteller tells a hypnotic story, metaphor, or teaching tale.

When the story crosses over the first threshold this is an isomorphic metaphor, in a sense; paralleling the exemplification of the bypassing of the subject's critical faculty. After this happens, the subject is entering the hypnotic state, where suggestions, can be given, without the possibility of rejection.

The Belly of the Whale

After crossing over the first threshold the protagonist disappears from what was his/her reality, before. Now, the character engulfed into the new world; namely, a new reality altogether, and one that is unknown, mythical, magical, illusory, and dreamlike.

Now, consider this for a moment. When I stop to consider this aspect of the classic story, I'm reminded of a dream, and also of childhood, where imaginations run wild and rampant; like an unbroken horse, refusing to be broken and force to comply with the way of the world.

For this reason, stories are the perfect vehicle for hypnosis, because they permit us to revert back to childhood, when we felt safe and protected from the fears and concerns adults have plenty of, where it's okay to play pretend and make believe, and use our imaginations impractically. Fun is allowed; yet, so is mental experientialism. In this way we're permitted to inspire and be inspired to create, preserve, and even destroy life as we choose; knowing anything is possible, and everything and everyone can be reborn into the Samsara of our own inner-world—where a story becomes alive—in a place I name the 'Other Mind'.

Stopping to reflect on the beginning up to now: The normal world is a metaphor for our ever day lives. The crossing over into the new world, i.e. the belly of the whale, is a metaphor for unconsciousness and the state that hypnosis is.

The Road of Trials

Now in the new world, the protagonist must face some trials: He/she must overcome some obstacles which stand between him/her and the sought-after boon. In Paulo Coelho's *The Alchemist*, the boon was the treasure the young shepherd boy went in search for; finding it, eventually, where he began his journey. In order to discover his personal legend, and discover his treasure, the young shepherd boy Santiago had to overcome many trials along his journey. Trials that made it easy for him to want to turn back to the life of a shepherd; forgetting the hardships he'd already endured, and make him want to forget his personal legend.

Trials are metaphors for problems.

When a hypnotherapy client, or potential customer, or anyone for that matter we encounter with a problem, comes to us, seeking help, we sometimes the most empowering way to help them is by presenting them with an isomorphic metaphor which solves a protagonist's problem. By doing this, the unconscious mind of that individual accesses resources the conscious mind might not have considered. Insights spark, and inspiration happens—like magic.

To think, a fairy-tale can solve a problem, and, yet, all the critical thinking in the world might fail a person. Interesting, isn't it?

In a religious epic a problem can be blown way out of proportion; the solution an incredible test of endurance and of illogical proportion and magnitude: Be careful though, because it might just inspire you to resolve through great empowerment and personal power to be relentless in overcoming your own seemingly insoluble problems. Actually, let's rethink this for a moment: maybe your problems now are perceived as benign; undoubtedly able to be resolved by fraction to the story. If you can perceive that anything is possible, then it makes problems appear much smaller than you might have originally observed them being.

A problem solved seems pale by comparison—even insignificant in some cases. I'm remembered of college days. I wanted to graduate with a 4.00 GPA. Each class, seemed like a giant obstacle standing in the way of my goal. One by one I defeated the monsters. After graduating with a 4.00 GPA I looked back and thought, "It really wasn't as brutal as I made it out to be, at first thought." My perception had changed, but what of the perception of the fresh student entering behind my graduation? Would the trials seem larger than life to them? I think so.

The journey is not only trails which must be overcome; it is also a glimpse of beauties unseen, understood not, and moments of spiritual awakenings—which make the journey worth the price of admission—one might argue.

The Meeting with the Goddess

This is the zenith of the story, which may bring goose bumps to your skin; a place in the story where the protagonist meets a higher divine power that gives him ultimately more power and a wholeness to be able to carry forth the requirements of the quest to completion. I think of this as an inner strength, stemming from a higher divine reason for completing the final tasks that await the hero/heroine.

If a hero, then usually this divine person is represented as a feminine divinity. If a heroine, then usually this divine person is represented as a masculine divinity. This is usually the missing link which keeps the hero from gaining the greatest self-confidence and personal power possible. When the hero is united with the Goddess, he's transitioned to being immortal, metaphorically.

In many ways this is an aspect of ourselves which has been lost, but which is now found, and an aspect that supercharges us and refocuses us back onto the mission in front of us. It's an inner power, represented by a character.

This archetype is very hypnotic in nature, because she's representative of our spiritual core; that is, our True Nature. When your subject realizes this archetype inside themselves, through your hypnotic stories, something shakes the ground beneath them and causes them to realize something so insightful that they're permanently changed, for the most part.

Woman as the Temptress

Don't be confused and think this is about gender, it's not. The archetype of the temptress is usually a female figure, but doesn't have to be. Temptation is the easy allurement of objects, people, and even places, which seek to stand in the way of our objectives, i.e. the purpose of our journey.

In Coelho's *The Alchemist* this could be the young Bedouin girl, Santiago has fallen in love with. Her beauty alone tempts him, making him even consider foregoing his destiny. This type of archetype is found in many other epics and myths one might explore.

The reality is that the temptress is a temporary pleasure one become affixed to; however, there cannot be any long term value derived, only short term value.

In many ways this archetype serves to test the purity and strength of the hero/heroine to determine if he/she is capable to move forward and complete the journey. Some fall captive to such illusiveness.

The parallel could be a strong relationship two people vow to uphold; yet, one that is fated when one partner breaks the eternal promise, for a short term pleasure with a stranger, to end the love relationship forever. It's a test of love and character.

The Atonement with the Father

A father represents control. In many stories, a father figure stands in the way of the hero/heroine taking over control and being able to sit at the head of the table, metaphorically speaking.

The relationship with the father often is a strained relationship. It often is one of competition and a battle for power and recognition.

Atonement with the father means standing up against the father and in some cases reconciling the relationship; putting it in a new light, one of equality or transference of power. Atonement of the father can also be reparation of an ideal or idea that stands in the way of the hero/heroine's future success.

Atonement of the father, in some stories, can be a standing up to God, or some higher god-like being. In this way atonement with the father can be a test of manhood, or a coming of age, or age of independence.

The Apotheosis

The woman as temptress and the atonement with the father are examples of trials the protagonist must overcome. These trials and possibly others elevate the hero/heroine to a new status. The word apotheosis literally translates to elevation to that of the gods; however, in our hypnotic stories this can actually be a higher elevated position in which the main character becomes strengthened in order to be able to carry forth the more unyielding task to come; namely, the grand mission, which is the most difficult trial yet to come.

In many storylines the main character may be portrayed in a different light, to make this point significant. In the Karate Kid, part 1, the protagonist Daniel Laruso, is given a headband, after he's endured the punishment of swept leg, by his opponent. He's then ready to face his opponent head on, delivering the famous Crane Kick that wins him the victory title.

These moments in the story really real in our attention, excite our emotions, and in many ways we become the character instead of merely the spectator watching the movie or reading the book. We become one with the hero, and their victory is our victory, or at the very least we become inspired and motivated to reengage in the pursuit of following after our dreams.

The Ultimate Boon

The ultimate boon is what the protagonist has risked life and limb to achieve. It is not only a physical object, magic elixir of life, an alchemy formula, or anything else most people would kill for if they believed they could have it; rather, it's a representations, a symbol of virtue, of strength—a symbol representing the entire journey. It's a trophy in many ways signifying the endurance, and intercourse in which the protagonist has had to deal with and overcome. It also represents change and success. The main point is it has more than just the value most place on it; it has intrinsic value that far supersedes the value anyone other human being could place on it.

For Daniel Laruso it was a symbol of accomplishing the impossible, while also a symbol of his annihilation of fear that robbed him of having what he wanted. For Santiago in The Alchemist is was symbolic of his journey and a symbol of transformation from that of being a mere shepherd boy into a true alchemist. For the protagonist the value of the ultimate boon is one of pricelessness. The invaluableness of the boon is proof of what the hero/heroine is made of and what cannot be taken away.

Often when someone recalls their happiest moment in life it can be associated with such an accomplishment of obtaining the ultimate boon; that is, their symbol of ultimate self-worth. You can watch their face become animated, their voice change to one of excitement, and you'll watch them take on an inner strength that is anchored to the experience—almost like they're reliving the experience all over again.

When you're reciting the hypnotic hero's journey and you get to this part in the story the other mind starts to make parallel associations with similar boons achieved by the subject. It may be conscious to where they break in to tell you about a similar journey they've been through, or it may be an unconscious recognition that becomes obvious to you they're experiencing when you observe their non-verbal behavior.

One thing is certain, you are affecting your hypnotic subject in a deeply resounding way mentally. This echoing of intense emotion that won't stop is causing a shift in them that is profoundly empowering and motivational. Their emotions are helping to change their state of mind and in return is bound to change their behavior and the types of decisions they will make in the future. These decisions will be confident, firm, and without hesitation; all pointing toward the direction of your desired outcome, which must parallel congruently the direction you're leading them toward.

People who are fearful of change, fearful of taking action, hesitant, who resist taking risks, will be freed from this disease, and will be more likely to travel the path you're mentally creating for them with your hypnotic story.

The Refusal of the Return

We have to think in terms of two worlds: (a) the world where the hero/heroine has emerged; namely the normal world, and (b) also the new world; the world which has altered him/her and elevated and changed him/her to something bigger than life. At this point in the story, the character is usually required to take the boon back to the normal world from whence he/she came for the betterment of humanity. The problem is the main character, now elevated, may not wish to return to the old way of life.

This creates an enigma of sorts given the character didn't want to leave the old world originally, and now doesn't want to leave the new world. It is a parallel that happens to the character, and in many ways the same emotions carry. Now the protagonist has become an individual, respected by others, and has a unique identity; whereas before he/she was identified with the community, the collectivistic qualities that had their own unique value. This situation puts the main character in a quagmire in which the natural response is to resist going home.

The Magic Flight

Not always, yet sometimes it may be that the boon is so valuable and so jealously guarded by a group or by the 'gods' that the hero/heroine must plan an escape to successfully get out of the path of danger in one piece.

The more valuable the boon, the more likely the main character will need to seek it and him/herself. Others will be swift to take the boon, especially if the protagonist has defeated a real threat that had guarded it for so long, and now the dangers that lurk do not perceive the protagonist as a great a threat. This may be an opportunity for others desiring the boon to take possession of it.

This can add another dimension of intrigue and vexation to the plot, and even a surprise ending; albeit one that is likely infuriating to the captive audience or your subject.

The Rescue From Without

It could be that when your protagonist character escapes the dangers lurking that in the process he/she is wounded, or significantly maimed. This is a bit ironic, because just as the protagonist found it necessary to have wise counsel and support in entering the new world, now the same character may need help exiting the new world in order to safely return back home to the normal world.

In such a case the main character after battling the antagonist, i.e. arch nemesis will somehow get some support from somewhere or someone that leads him/her safely back to home. This could be a great transition back to normalcy, especially given the main character may not want to leave the new world to return back home. This could be what reunites the protagonist with the old world.

In the motion picture *The Wizard of Oz* Dorothy clicks the heels of her ruby red slippers and finds herself back home as if it had all been nothing more than a dream—leaving her possibly doubting the existence of the whole new world Oz, altogether.

There are so many creative ways to bring the main character back to reality, or the old normal world, that it can make for a really great experience for the captive audience. As you tell your hypnotic stories keep this in mind, because you may find inspiration coming to you the more you tell such stories. You can also begin to get a sense of different types ending do to your subject mentally.

The purpose of course is to achieve the outcome from your story that you seek. In most instances this will be to have your hypnotic subjects complying with your post-hypnotic commands.

The Crossing of the Return Threshold

The return threshold holds as much significance as the entry or first threshold; the difference being that instead of a symbolic entrance into the unexplored unconscious 'other mind' now the hero returns to the conscious everyday world that represents home, safety, and union back with the familiar. This reentry into the home-zone is reentry back into the 'real' world for the hero/heroine.

Sometimes a story will conclude one last battle right before the hero/heroine leaves the new world headed back to the old world from whence he/she's come.

Upon returning the metamorphosis is usually only understood by the protagonist: like was the case of *The Wizard of Oz* where Dorothy awakens back in Kansas. Her family didn't see or understand the transformation which had taken place in Dorothy, but she did. This can be a difficult readjustment for the character, and in some stories the protagonist may be deemed an outcast, or there may be some great mental distress that causes a depression to fall on the main character.

I am remembered of a journey I personally took once. I had left the United States and ventured off to India while in my teens. I went there alone, feeling a spiritual calling to do so. I went through the gamut of the hero's journey, experiencing a foreign land and underwent a major transformation while there. When I returned people observed me as I were before I left, which was vastly different than the me that observed me then. I fell into a great depression, wishing I was back in India, and feeling as though I was disconnected with a part of myself.

That was years ago; however, my point for sharing this story is to emphasis the point that Jesus makes when he says in the New Testament:

> *"A prophet is not without honour, but in his own country, and among his own kin, and in his own house."—Jesus*

You see, people only know the 'you' they know while in your company. The company you kept in the new world see you in one light and characterization, while the people in the old world see you as you were before you left. It is a strange phenomenon if you ever get the opportunity to experience it.

The Master of Two Worlds

So much of hypnosis deals with this idea of inner and outer worlds; namely, the 'mind' and the 'other mind' or 'conscious mind' and 'unconscious mind'. The 'hypnotic' hero's journey is representative of this mastery of both worlds.

As a hypnotic storyteller you're taking people in and out of conscious and unconscious states known as fractionation. Each time you takes someone back to the old world from the new world you're essentially taking them out of hypnosis and back to the 'real' world.

Hypnosis of course occurs naturally every 90 – 120 minutes of our waking day; a phenomenon known as circadian rhythms. During this cycle we experience zoning out into trance, or daydreaming, which takes us out of consciousness and into the world of our 'other mind' or unconscious mind.

In a story, the protagonist comes to understand these two dimensions of him/herself equally—mastering both! The human condition is to experience stories and become transported into these foreign worlds. In persuasion psychology 'Narrative Transportation Theory' is this very act by which we assume the identity of the protagonist and empathize with the main character. We leave our conscious world to enter the 'unknown' to experience life aside from the known and familiar.

Stories are naturally hypnotic; yet, when the hypnotic storyteller adds in extra layers of hypnotic machinations the captive audience, i.e. your hypnotic subjects are put under the spell of hypnosis to the extent that you are able to communicate with them on multiple levels and to meet certain outcome objectives.

There are many benefits to hypnotic storytelling: (a) they build deep rapport, (b) they communicate indirectly without raising suspicion or doubt, (c) they suspend judgments, (d) they allow you to communicate eloquently and in a way people will embrace listening to you, and (e) the let you hypnotize your subject without them knowing they are being hypnotized.

In my opinion hypnotic storytelling is one of the most fascinating means by which to hypnotize others. The very hypnotic nature of stories make them one of my preferred means to hypnotize my subjects covertly. When I worked in sales, there was a cliché that went: "Facts fail; stories sell!" This simply meant that people buy the emotional benefits that come by way of the story they tell themselves or hear from the sales professional; rather, than from the logical advantages, i.e., facts about the attributes a product possesses.

Stories are told to us when we're children as we're being lulled to sleep by our parents; a form of childhood hypnosis, in terms of process. As a child resting in a parents arms, we're presented with a story to distract our conscious mind from outside, real-world, activities, and in this way we're dissociating from 'reality' as we're rocked to sleep, rhythmically, by both the lulling of our parents rocking back and forth movement, and the gently whispered words that do for us what a college professor's monotone tone does, which is to send us into the hypnotic state; where we find ourselves naturally experiencing just before sleep at night. "Sweet dreams!" may be the last words spoken to us, yet it's likely we're asleep long before we'll consciously hear them. It's true, telling stories has many benefits.

The Freedom to Live

This is the last dimension to Campbell's 'Hero's Journey'. For the hypnotic storyteller, this is the last dimension of the classic story that will serve as the base from which to later add in many hypnotic elements (e.g., hypnotic language patterns, embedded commands, etc.).

This final aspect spells freedom for the protagonist character. The hero/heroine is able to slip into and out of the two realities as they choose. At a level of mastery, gained from experience, the hero/heroine may become a teacher, or guide, to future adventurers. They have the knowledge and the know-how to advise others about the two worlds, and to inspire and promote both realms.

The adventure may become in time a myth or an epic tale that gets passed down from one generation to the next. In this way the protagonist may be elevated by others to the level of a god. The hero thus becomes someone to be looked up to by future generations of youth aspiring to achieve the same status.

The hypnotic storyteller will want to understand this very carefully, because as you tell your hypnotic story this last leg of the story will create hope and possibility in the mindset of your subject; namely, the subject who has not come face to face yet with his/her own personal legend. In so many ways this will be an encouragement for your subject to take action; that is, a motivator for them to want to take action –and, while in this mindset, <u>any action</u> can be put forward—for example, the outcome you desire from them, and in return complied.

What If You Are Unable to Remember All of This Straightaway?

I ask you not to fret over learning all seventeen steps of Campbell's 'Hero's Journey' as it's not necessary now that you must do so. Recognizing the common thread that runs through most stories is the main point for teaching you this model.

My adaptation of this model, calling it: 'The Hypnotic Hero's Journey' is to point out to you the symbols that are representations of the 'hypnotic' process and even what I understand 'hypnosis' to be experientially. These are things like the bypassing of the critical faculty in which the character represents the hypnotic subject in that they forego critical thinking, opting to suspend their disbelief, and preferring to take a leap of faith, and let down their guard, to take a chance on journeying into the 'unknown'; that is, representative of the 'other mind' or the 'emotional mind' or what some might refer to as the 'unconscious mind'. In my mind, I refer to this as they 'other mind' or the 'hypnotic mind'. There are so many parallels that I have pointed out that it is enough you simply generalize these parallels.

In the immediacy, you, the learner, are only required to know that parallels exist between the juxtaposition of a 'story' and what is 'hypnosis'. I'm from the school of thought that believes that all learning is heuristic and learned first 'unconsciously', which in time becomes learned critically or 'consciously'. What I'm suggesting to you is that you already have learned this model through your unconscious experiences having told many stories you've modeled innately from this model. To be more candid: You already know the 'Hypnotic Hero's Journey' apart from knowing you know it or not.

The Recap

This chapter took you through the Monomyth that was originally modelled by Joseph Campbell, from his book: *The Hero with a Thousand Faces*. This is the classic story plot that runs common throughout most myths and epic adventures.

I adapted this original model to relay to you the hypnotic parallels that set the stage for hypnotic storytelling convention. The structure of the hypnotic hero's journey bridges from the critical conscious mind over into the unknown mysteries of the unconscious mind. This cross over parallels the hypnotic induction process. At the gates where stands the journey the critical faculty must be bypassed, paralleling Campbell's 'First Threshold' step. Once bypassed, the journey begins, or in our case 'the hypnosis' in which the 'hypnotic mind' is traversed through the hypnotic subject's imagination and ability to play make believe and pretend with their other mind. This guiding process is parallel to that of the story told from one step to another onward. All the while the hypnotic subject is being taken on a long journey of secrecy and excitement; yet, without the hypnotic subject consciously having to travel anywhere.

Emotions are affected by the plot of the hypnotic story changing minds and the propensity that the hypnotic subject will comply more probabilistically with the hypnotist's indirect suggestions. The likelihood of the desired outcome is sooner reached when the hypnotic story is applied.

The Next Step

Academically, I can tell you the step-by-step logic of the psychological principles applied to hypnotic storytelling; however, I know it wouldn't make you a better hypnotic storyteller.

As I've mentioned I believe that learning comes by doing, and testing for yourself the lessons in this book. I think all learning first happens at the unconscious level, and that the conscious mind takes more time to catch up to what you already have learnt unconsciously, already.

With hypnotic storytelling you have already inside you the knowledge and learnings to be able to capably well tell hypnotic stories. In truth, you already tell hypnotic stories without even being aware when you do.

This book walks you through the process of hypnotic storytelling in a unique way that brings with it clarity. It is better not to overthink hypnotic storytelling, because as soon as you do, you stop being quite so hypnotic.

These exercises will help prepare you to tell hypnotic stories without your critical thinking getting in the way. The 'hypnotic mind' is the 'other mind' which has already learnt the Hypnotic Hero's Journey Model, I've presented to you. I ask you to suspend your disbelief and trust in the process, and let your stories hypnotize your subjects naturally. Consider this blind faith in your 'hypnotic mind' comparable to riding a bicycle you've already learned to ride. You might at any moment mount a bicycle in the future and ride it without your conscious mind's interference—brilliantly!

Have a think about that as you become astonished by your 'hypnotic mind's' ability to affect real change in others—gaining you what you want.

I.   Mentally reflect on the Hypnotic Hero's Journey: (a) broadly consider the normal reality people live in consciously every single day, (b) think about the challenges that confront us whenever we want to step outside our comfort zones (e.g., mental hiccups, and physical limitations), (c) remember the trials we are faced with when embarking on the journey of unexplored territories, (d) recall what it feels like to accomplish a mighty goal of impossibility, and (e) picture how you're perceived by others upon returning to the old environment, which may pale in comparison to the changes which have occurred inside you.

II.   Think up an imaginative story without giving much thought to it; that is, let the process flow creatively and inspirationally. Your inspirations come from your 'hypnotic mind'. Notice if you start to leave your conscious world and enter the world of the 'other mind', i.e. 'hypnotic mind'. Decide how that feels; this transformation.

III.   Tell your story to a random stranger when the appropriate time presents itself. You don't want to tell your story when someone is to be back on the job shortly. Remember, these stories are hypnotic and should not be shared when your subject will be required to operate machinery or drive a vehicle. Safety first always, please!

CHAPTER 3

REALITY IS PLASTIC

eality is something most of us take for granted. This chapter will focus on the linguistic aspects of how we construct reality with our language which gets rationalized perceptually. Again, I want to ask you to suspend your doubts about what I'm going to teach you and allow yourself to have an open mind. Elsewise, you might get real confused, real quick.

The importance of understanding how we use language to explain a conceptual reality is the value that lets you create hypnotic realities whenever you want to; namely, using hypnotic storytelling.

When we think of the external world we observe with our five senses; that is, the 'objects' we perceive of as reality. More precisely we observe the 'objects' of the world in relation to space, time, energy, and matter. Space is the distance and location an object is located in relation to another object. Time is a linear relationship in terms of the age of an object. Energy is the quality or the attributes that define an object. Matter is the material nature of an object.

Think about something astonishing for a moment: Consider that our language is constructed, systematically, to represent reality perceptually. Take any something around you—for example, a 'pen'. The pen is considered to be matter. Where is the pen? Let's imagine it was on the desk some months back. What type of pen was it? Let's pretend it was a really black pen, with shiny gold embellishments.

Now this example is a make believe example; however, were it 'real'; that is, part of your 'reality' then you'd understand the reality through various predicates: (a) matter predicate (e.g., 'something'), (b) space predicate (e.g., 'on' the desk), (c) time predicate (e.g., 'some' months ago), and (d) energy predicate (e.g., 'really' black … 'shiny' gold…).

The object observed is a pen, but it's in relation to a space; meaning it's an adverb 'on' that tells us where the object is in relation to a defined space. The verb 'was' tells us at some point in the past the pen was 'on' the desk. We don't have enough information to know if it is 'still' on the desk. It could be that the pen is 'now' 'behind' the desk; that is maybe it fell, and is now located in a different space from what it was at a previous time when it was 'on' the desk. Again, we don't know. The pen could be any pen, but we have information that tells us that the pen is of a certain quality having specified attributes which define it in relation to other pens that may have been previously and currently in our experience. In this case the pen is 'really' black; that is, not 'just' black, but 'really' black. It is also a 'shiny' gold, not a 'dull' gold. Shiny is an energy predicate that defines the characteristic of the gold embellishments.

If you'll keep these four characteristics of reality in mind, you'll be able to create realities in your subject's mind, and your stories will be richer and more eloquent.

Why are Space, Time, Energy, and Matter Predicates Important for the Hypnotic Storyteller?

It is important to understand the four reality predicates because being well versed in the corresponding linguistic representations of each, will let you brilliantly craft your stories eloquently so you will instantly captivate the attention of your subject in order to hypnotize them more immediately.

Matter is essentially 'some' 'specific' object. The word 'some' is an adjective as well as 'specific'; explicitly, these words give an orientation to the noun. There are many choices which could have worked to qualify the noun—for example, 'any' object, or 'whichever' object. Each of these adjectives restricts the noun narrowing the ambiguity surrounding the object, in order to bring clarity to the object.

Energy is the unique attributes the object possesses. These attributes make the object unique and help to create a mental impression in the mind of the subject that is narrower in focus. I think the easiest way to consider energy predicates is to think of the interrogative word 'how'; because, 'how' asks the question: How is this distinguished qualitatively from something similar, but not the same.

These energy predicates are adverbs. Adverbs vastly consists of words that end in *–ly* (e.g., attractively, amicably, totally, completely, etc.); in spite of that, this isn't always the case (e.g., enough, more than, to the extent, etc.). These energy predicates create a different experience in the mind of the subject. Interestingly, these adverbs can be real similar, yet still create a different experience.

Consider this for yourself by thinking about the following three adverbial clauses that are nearly the same, but not exactly: (a) 'anyhow', (b) 'anyway', and (c) 'at any rate'. Notice the subtle differences?

It helps to put them in a context: (a) Anyhow, we'll leave tomorrow, (b) Anyway, we'll leave tomorrow, and (c) At any rate, we'll leave tomorrow. These nuances may seem insignificant, but I'm preparing you to be a world-class hypnotic storyteller, and believe me when I tell you, that each of these three adverbial clauses take the subject down the road to a different experience. By taking the time to learn these experiences beforehand you for the most part have the experiences to be able to share with your subjects—knowing firsthand yourself what experiences your language creates.

Time is linear. There's the past, the present, and the future. The past is something we're associated with, simply because it's permanent and fixed. You cannot go back in time and change the past. For some people the past is a comfortable place because it represents the 'known'. The future time is more dissociative in nature; that is, we're not guaranteed a specific future, and the future, because it hasn't occurred, is subject to change. The future represents the 'unknown'.

As is the case with energy predicates, time predicates take on certain variants of adverbs, yet, ones associated with time (e.g., before, afterward, yet, now, late, early, subsequently, successively, etc.). If you revisit our 'pen' example, you'll notice the time predicates 'some' and 'ago' (e.g., "…some months ago…"). The predicate adverb 'some' could have easily been replaced with 'a few' or 'more or less' or 'several'. The predicate adverb 'ago' could have been replaced with 'in the past' or 'before' or even 'since'. Take a minute to moment to consider the possible sequences and notice the subtle differences between each of these time sequences.

- …more or less months in the past…

- …several months since…

- …a few months before…

- …more or less months since…

- …several months before…

- …a few months in the past…

- …more or less months before…

- ...several months in the past...

- ...a few months since...

These are a few sequences of the time predicates being used to help you consider the differences in perception your hypnotic subject might experience mentally. Predicates are words that enrich language. When learning a language it is natural that someone will learn a basic vocabulary of nouns and simple verbs—for example, 'I hungry'. This is fine for beginner; however, it is clear that the person using such language is a novice at communicating in that particular language. At some future point, the learner masters language to the extent they capably use predicates to ground the language and make it more coherent and to reference an object to another object in space, another point in time, or even a difference in quality.

Space is a location where an object is located in time—for example, our pen is located 'on' the desk some months ago. Notice it's not 'beneath' the desk; nor is it 'under' the desk; nor is it 'underneath' the desk; nor is it even 'lower than' the desk. No! It's 'on' the desk; not 'above' the desk; not 'hovering over' the desk; nor is it 'on top of' the desk. No! It's simply 'on' the desk. Do you perceive the various meta-categories of possibility?

Can you start to get the differences of these various possibilities which could have been used? When you think of the word 'on' you might equate its opposite as being 'off'. If the pen is not 'on' the desk, then it probably gets assumed to be 'off' the desk. If the pen isn't 'above' the desk, then it might make you think that the pen is 'below' the desk. Is it conceivable to think that the pen is simply being used at present moment; that is, 'in' hand?

Now perhaps you're beginning to see why these predicates are so important for creating hypnotic story realities. The linguistic constructs parallel reality; yet, also allows you the freedom and flexibility to create certain mental experiences in the mind of your subject. Painting a picture and as well as an experience in the mind of your hypnotic subject is critical for telling the deepest spellbinding stories.

What Makes Space, Time, Energy, and Matter Predicates Extremely Hypnotic?

Besides being the foundation of all reality as we perceive it with our five senses, when you use these predicates, you're often using language in a way that communicates on multiple levels. Evoke what is meant when I say:

> *"In some measure, beyond what I was led to believe, the whole enchilada is nothing more than a tiny tasteless morsel—though still outside of what I had to eat prior to before it was handed to me on a late plate."*

Confused? Have you figured it out, yet?

If you haven't it is quite alright. The point is that it is ambiguous enough standing on its own, though without a proper context, it is impossible to know for certain what this eluding statement really means. Some might assume it to be a metaphor judging what some prize as 'the whole enchilada', while others may think this is a dining experience a food critic is putting down poetically.

Such a wooly statement can be too complex to figure out; especially, because the critical faculty, as previously mentioned, can only process 7+/-2 bits of information at any given time. While the critical mind is trying to process such a statement, the hypnotic storyteller has already covertly embedded post-hypnotic suggestions using analogue marking. Now, the subject is playing catch-up, meaning they're jumping ahead, to where the storyteller is at now, but in the process of doing so is deleting much information, and generalizing what they think the storyteller has intentioned.

The story becomes hypnotic because the subject is preconditioned to certain patterns. We all have an idea of what we think reality should look like. Our critical minds are a wonderful part of the brain that processes language, sequences, and patterns, making it unnecessary that we should have to relearn everything afresh each passing day, or have to consciously think about doing every task that comes before us. This brain habitually follows patterns that have been etched in the brain through repetition. The critical mind is there to protect us from all the information that is constantly bombarding us. Once we learn something consciously we can simply let our brains process the patterns without much critical thinking necessary.

Wouldn't it be rather weird to have to consciously think about dressing yourself each morning when you awake, or to think about making a phone call, or to think long and hard about how to drive to work each morning? Thankfully, we don't have to do this, because of our hypnotic patterns, which let us operate hypnotically when it pertains to tasks we do repetitively and regularly.

If you somehow find yourself looking in the mirror and notice your shirt is on backwards, such a pattern interrupt may have you wondering how that happened, and in which case you may decide to be more conscious about putting your clothes on and how you move throughout the rest of your day. You may blame the unconscious mistake on not having gotten enough sleep, or some other reason to seek to make sense of the oversight, and this excuse may have you believing that you'll make other slipups if you don't pay attention to what's going on around you.

In such a case driving yourself to work may be a real challenge as you overthink your driving abilities. Yet, why do I mention all this? I mention it, because people are conditioned to comply with patterns, because these patterns are habits that make life easier. Linguistically, we're conditioned to follow along with a story, because we unconsciously do it all the time. What happens when the hypnotic storyteller uses language in a way that interrupts your pattern, however? The answer: The same thing that happens when you mistakenly slipup and put your shirt on backward. You become confused about what's going on, critically try to make sense of it, but in the end, end up completely hypnotized, because you're unable to focus on other important tasks around you. This is the classic hypnotic pattern-interrupt.

The four predicates are some of the most potently hypnotic language patterns that can quickly, without warning, send the critical faculty out to lunch, while the hypnotic storyteller weaves in his/her hypnotic suggestions.

How to Master the Hypnotic Language of Reality to Instantly Pattern Plastic Realities Intended for Your Hypnotic Subjects?

In order to create hypnotic realities that are believable and which change minds and affect people hypnotically, you must first master these hypnotic language predicates. The way to master them is by experiencing them yourself and getting a feel for how others might experience them likewise. It is no guarantee that anyone will experience reality exactly as you experience it; yet, it is conceivable to think that generally speaking most people will experience it in a broad sense the same as you will.

The first step is observing broadly what each predicate represents in terms of your external reality. This means understanding that time is a linear progression, objects, i.e., matter, are situated in space, and that matter has attributes that characterize it from other matter.

The second step is looking past mere nouns and simple verbs; namely, observing the predicates that distinguish where an object is in reference to other matter, the quality of the matter, and the relationship the matter has with time.

The third step is identifying the predicates and considering possible replacements for the predicates to determine if it makes more sense or less sense using the alternative predicates.

If I say: "A while back, I noticed a blue camera, sitting aside next to a slowly moving tortoise walking along the beach." Deconstructing this sentence right away we see that 'A while back' is a reference to time, next is an 'identity' and 'awareness' predicate (e.g., I noticed), then is a blue camera, which is an object, next we find a space predicate (e.g., sitting aside next to), that is referencing the camera to the location of a moving turtle, but wait, the turtle is moving 'slowly' which is an energy predicate, as it is the quality of the turtle's walk, and next we find another space predicate, which is 'along' as it is referencing the turtles position by comparing it to the beach's position in space.

It's a good idea to practice deconstructing language in the way I have done above; namely, taking notice of all the variations of predicate patterns that exist and which can be used when telling your hypnotic stories. It is also worth mentioning that you can use these language predicates to also speak for hypnotically while engaging in seemingly innocent conversations with others, covertly, and indirectly.

To make this process easier for you, and give you a leg up in hypnotically creating reality for others while you tell your tell hypnotic stories, I've already deconstructed many predicates for you, and categorized them into the four linguistic predicate types that define reality. All you have to do is simply study these patterns, adding to them new ones you decode yourself, and you can instantly improve your ability to speak hypnotically while creating plastic realities for your subjects.

Space Predicates

- Above ___
- Above your head ___
- Along ___
- Along with ___
- Alongside ___
- Amid ___
- Among ___
- Amongst ___
- Anyhow ___
- Anyplace ___
- Anyway ___
- Anyways ___
- Apart ___
- Apart from ___
- Around ___
- Aside (from) ___
- At hand ___
- At the side of ___
- At this juncture ___
- At this place ___
- At this point ___
- Atop ___
- Away ___
- Below ___
- Beneath ___
- Beside ___
- Between ___
- Beyond ___
- Bordering ___
- Close by ___
- Combined with ___
- Concerning ___
- Connecting ___
- Contained by ___
- Directly above ___
- Everywhere ___
- Exceeding ___
- Far from ___
- Flanking ___
- Greater than ___
- Here ___
- Higher than ___

- However ___
- In ___
- In conjunction with ___
- In front ___
- In place of ___
- In reserve ___
- In the air ___
- In the bounds of ___
- In the interior ___
- In the middle of ___
- Indoors ___
- Inside ___
- Involving ___
- Joining ___
- Less ___
- Linking ___
- Lower ___
- Lower than ___
- More than ___
- Near ___
- Near ___
- Near by ___
- Next to ___
- Not more than ___
- Notwithstanding ___
- O'er ___
- On the side ___
- On top of ___
- On top of ___
- Out of the way ___
- Outside ___
- Over ___
- Over head ___
- Overhead ___
- Past ___
- Sandwiched between ___
- Separately ___
- Sideways ___
- Sideways ___
- Sidewise ___
- Somewhere ___
- Stuck between ___
- Surrounded by ___
- There ___
- To one side ___
- To the left ___
- To the right ___
- To the side ___

- Together with ___
- Under ___
- Underneath ___

- Up your sleeve ___
- Where ___
- Wherever ___
- Within ___

Time Predicates

- 'till ___
- Afore ___
- After ___
- After ___ Towards ___
- Afterward ___
- Afterwards ___
- Ago ___
- Ahead ___
- All through ___
- Almost immediately ___
- Already ___
- Although ___
- Anon ___
- Anytime ___
- As ___
- As of ___
- At an earlier time ___
- At once ___
- At present ___

- At some point in ___
- At some stage in ___
- At the moment ___
- At the present ___
- At the same time as ___
- At this instance ___
- At this moment ___
- At this point ___
- At this time ___
- Back ___
- Because ___
- Before ___
- Before ___
- Before long ___
- Before now ___
- Beforehand ___

- Beforehand ___
- Beginning ___
  Commencing
  ___
- But ___
- But then again
  ___
- By now ___
- By this time ___
- Completed ___
- Currently ___
- Despite the time
  when ___
- During ___
- During which
  ___
- Earlier ___
- En route for ___
- Even as ___
- Even now ___
- Even though ___
- Ever since ___
- Finished ___
- For the duration
  of ___
- For the period of
  ___
- Formerly ___
- Formerly ___
- From ___ To ___

- From the time
  when ___
- Given that ___
- Gone ___
- Headed for ___
- Hitherto ___
- However ___
- Immediately ___
- In ___
- In a jiffy ___
- In a little while
  ___
- In a while ___
- In advance ___
- In advance ___
- In contrast ___
- In course of ___
- In half a shake
  ___
- In next to no
  time ___
- In spite of that
  ___
- In spite of that
  ___
- In spite of this
  ___
- In the direction
  of ___

- In the meantime ___
- In the past ___
- In the past ___
- In the past ___
- In view of the fact that ___
- Just before ___
- Later ___
- Later ___
- Later ___
- Later on ___
- Later than ___
- Meanwhile ___
- Momentarily ___
- Near when ___
- Next ___
- Next ___
- Now ___
- Nowadays ___
- On or after ___
- Past ___
- Past ___
- Pending ___
- Presently ___
- Presently ___
- Previously ___
- Previously ___
- Previously ___
- Promptly ___
- Pronto ___
- Quickly ___
- Rapidly ___
- Right away ___
- Right now ___
- Seeing as ___
- Shortly ___
- Shortly ___
- Since ___
- Since ___
- So far ___
- Soon ___
- Soon ___
- Soon after ___
- Sooner than ___
- Still ___
- Still ___
- Straightaway ___
- Straightway ___
- Subsequently ___
- Subsequently ___
- Then ___
- Though ___
- Through ___
- Through ___
- Throughout ___
- Throughout ___

- Thru ___
- Thus far ___
- Till ___
- Until ___
- Until now ___
- Until this time ___
- Up till now ___
- Up to ___
- Up until ___
- Whereas ___
- While ___
- While ___
- While waiting for ___
- Whilst ___
- Without hesitation ___
- Yet ___

Energy Predicates

- A lesser amount of ___
- A reduced amount of ___
- A smaller amount of ___
- Absolutely ___
- Abundantly ___
- Additional ___
- Additionally ___
- Adequately ___
- Agreed ___
- Alone ___
- Amply ___
- An adequate amount of ___
- Anyhow ___
- Anyway ___
- At any rate ___
- At least ___
- Barely ___
- Besides ___
- Categorically ___
- Certainly ___
- Completely ___
- Definitely ___
- Down right ___
- Enormously ___
- Enough ___
- Entirely ___
- Excluding ___
- Exclusively ___
- Extra ___
- Extremely ___
- Fewer ___
- Fewer than ___
- Finally ___

- From tip to toe ___
- From top to bottom ___
- Fully ___
- Fully ___
- Further ___
- Hardly ___
- In addition ___
- In any case ___
- In part ___
- In some measure ___
- Incompletely ___
- Just ___
- Just ___
- Just about ___
- Less than ___
- Merely ___
- Minus ___
- Moderately ___
- More than ___
- Nevertheless ___
- No more than ___
- No question ___
- Nonetheless ___
- Not as much of ___
- Now then ___

- Obviously ___
- Of course ___
- On top ___
- Only ___
- Partially ___
- Partly ___
- Perfectly ___
- Plentifully ___
- Plenty ___
- Simply ___
- Singularly ___
- So ___
- Solely ___
- Somewhat ___
- Sufficiently ___
- Take away ___
- Thoroughly ___
- To a degree ___
- To cut a long story short ___
- To some extent ___
- To spare ___
- To the amount ___
- To the degree ___
- To the extent ___
- To the level ___

- To the limit ___
- To the magnitude ___
- To the point ___
- To the potential ___
- To the range ___
- To the scope ___
- To the size ___
- Totally ___
- Totally ___
- Unconditionally ___
- Undeniably ___
- Unequivocally ___
- Unquestionably ___
- Utterly ___
- Utterly ___
- Very ___
- Well ___
- Wholly ___
- With a reduction of ___
- Without question ___

- Only just ___
- Scarcely ___
- In addition to ___
- Extra ___
- Extremely ___
- Very ___
- Awfully ___
- Enormously ___
- Exceedingly ___
- Exceptionally ___
- Particularly ___
- Really ___
- Tremendously ___
- Slightly ___
- Marginally ___
- Somewhat ___
- Faintly ___
- Vaguely ___
- A little ___
- A tad ___
- A touch ___
- To some extent ___

Matter Predicates

- A few ___

- A fraction of ___

- A job of ___
- A part of ___
- A piece of ___
- A portion of ___
- A role of ___
- A share of ___
- Added ___
- Additional ___
- Alike ___
- All ___
- All ___
- Any ___
- Any ___
- Anything ___
- Apart from ___
- Apiece ___
- Bar ___
- Barely ___
- Both ___
- But ___
- Consistent ___
- Constricted ___
- Each ___
- Each ___
- Each and every one ___
- Each one ___
- Equal ___
- Equivalent ___
- Erstwhile ___
- Even ___
- Every ___
- Every ___
- Every ___
- Every bit of ___
- Every one ___
- Every one of ___
- Every part ___
- Every part of ___
- Every single ___
- Every single one ___
- Everyone ___
- Everything ___
- Everything ___
- Except ___
- Except ___
- Except for ___
- Excepting ___
- Expanded ___
- Expanse ___
- Extra ___
- Fine ___
- First ___
- For each ___
- Former ___
- Fresh ___
- Identical ___
- Individual ___
- Individually ___

- Invariable ___
- Just ___
- Last ___
- Limited ___
- Lone ___
- Matching ___
- More ___
- Narrow ___
- Narrow down ___
- New ___
- No matter what ___
- No matter which ___
- No more than ___
- Not including ___
- Old ___
- One ___
- One and only ___
- Onetime ___
- Only ___
- Other ___
- Reduce ___
- Reduce down ___
- Respectively ___
- Restricted ___

- Save for ___
- Separately ___
- Several ___
- Several ___
- Similar ___
- Similar ___
- Simple ___
- Simply ___
- Single ___
- Slight ___
- Solitary ___
- Some ___
- Some ___
- Some ___
- Something ___
- Spread-Wider ___
- Tapered ___
- The complete ___
- The entire ___
- The lot ___
- The whole ___
- The whole ball of wax ___
- The whole bit and caboodle ___
- The whole en-chilada ___

- The whole lot ___

- The whole she-bang ___
- The whole things ___
- Tighten ___
- Tighten down ___

- Tightened ___
- To each ___
- Unaffected ___
- Unchanged ___
- Uniform ___
- Unique ___

- What different ___

- What else ___
- What new ___
- What old ___
- Whatever ___
- Whatever ___
- Whatever thing ___

- Whatsoever ___
- Whichever ___
- Wide-range ___
- Wide-spread ___
- With the exception of ___

You'll see evidence in these four lists to support how each of the predicates are used together to construct meanings more meaningfully—for example, you might construct: "Apart from the really now part the fearless character only narrowly grasps a moment to peacefully meditate above his time." Deconstructing this you'll notice the structure is comprised of matter predicates (e.g., part, character), space predicates (e.g., apart, narrowly, above), time predicates (e.g., now, moment, time), and energy predicates (e.g., really, fearless, peacefully). There's cross-over of uses that cause a mild hypnotic confusion to happen naturally—for example: "...really now..." and "...only narrowly grasps a moment..." When you stop to consider what a 'moment' is you might consider it a tangible object located in space; however, it's actually a temporal clause that defines a time limit—it's not actually matter, but it is used in this construction as though it were, however. The linguistic strategy behind this, which makes it very hypnotic, is the way that the word 'moment' is a characteristic of time that has been nominalized, i.e. turned into a noun, and used as though it were an object. When we naturally think of a noun we think of a 'person', 'place' or 'object'. In this construction time has been coded as an abstract noun named a 'moment'. We all communicate with abstraction at times. Though abstract nouns don't convey things we can experience with our senses – we can't feel, touch, see, hear, or taste them – they let us express important meaning, nonetheless.

Being able to recognize and use abstract nouns is important, especially for the purpose of communicating hypnotically. While abstract nouns can convey deep emotion, which is persuasively hypnotic, the hypnotic storyteller runs the risk of not clearly expressing his or her meaning when he wants to. Things get lost in translation so to speak. Since abstract words are by definition abstract, they can mean different things to different people, so take heed to make sure your writing and hypnotic stories only use concrete nouns for clarification only to the extent you want your stories to be less hypnotic. Generally speaking, sentences comprised largely of concrete nouns are more clear and concise; yet, not nearly so hypnotic. So revisiting the example I just provided you with, take notice of how artfully vague and hypnotic the construction is. It seems to make sense, and maybe it does to you, yet, only to the extent you let it to—get it?!!

Reality is constructed hypnotically when these four predicates are used to intentionally form abstract constructs. Interestingly, we can use the same predicates to form perceptual constructs that are perceived as real; that is, 'reality', because perception is acquired through the sensory system, i.e. seeing, feeling, listening, tasting, and smelling. These four predicates can create a solid argument for a concrete reality; yet, create a solid argument for how absent reality is or how plastic it is. Hypnotized, yet?

What if I Add Awareness Predicates to the Mix?

Being a hypnotic storyteller is a lot along the same lines as being an illusionist—only with words instead of slights of hand and magic props. A hypnotic storyteller is an expert wordsmith; yet, also a master of misdirection with the ability to focus or defocus his/her subject's attention anywhere or not that he/she intends for it to go.

You can construct whole new realities using sensory predicates that serve you linguistically, which let you create what is real and what is not—to describe the world as you wish for other to perceive it to be. These predicates, as we've learnt, also have the power to bewilder and cause our subjects to think of reality as disconcerting illusion, at best.

A sequence of the hypnotic process is to absorb attention. When you self-hypnotize yourself you can do this by focusing your attention on a spot on a wall, or focusing your attention on a candle flame until you achieve tunnel vision and enter a trance. There are many methods; however, attention must be focused to hypnotize someone.

How do we capture someone's awareness and focus it where we want it to go? The answer is to use awareness predicates. You simply cannot focus on everything in the field of sensory reality. You can only truly focus on between five to nine bits of information at any given moment. When too much comes at you too quickly in your brain miraculously rank-orders everything into what's most important for your wellbeing and filters out the rest. This is what we've labeled as the 'critical faculty' or the aspect of us which controls our 'critical thinking'. As a hypnotist I don't want you really over thinking things; rather, I want you, my subject, complying with my indirect suggestions. The easiest way for me to bend your will is to hypnotize you covertly merely by telling you a hypnotic story.

Controlling your awareness is important to me. If I can get you to thinking about something I want you to think about in a particular way, then it makes it so much easier on me, because I can assume in good faith that you'll comply with my wishes. Not to worry though, I'll give you an experience with my stories that will inspire you, astonish you, and have you feeling really terrific.

If I tell you not to think about a 'blue' elephant chances are you already have—which is great if my intent all along was to have you think about a blue elephant. What have I done by giving you that reversal frame? What I've done is capture your attention and focus it on the 'blue' elephant I wanted you thinking about. Want to or not you complied!

Linguistically certain predicates; namely 'awareness predicates', focus your hypnotic subject's attention astonishingly well.

As before, I'm going to give you a ton of awareness predicates that you can learn overtime to increase the range of your hypnotic linguistics. These language patterns are cookie-cutter templates that you may simply fill in the blank with whatever, wherever, however, or whenever direction you want to focus it. Incidentally, notice that the predicates: 'whatever', 'wherever', 'however', and 'whenever' are all representative of the four earlier predicates (e.g., matter, space, energy, and time) that people use to perceive reality as real. So, awareness predicates help you direct attention back onto the plastic realities you create in the minds of your hypnotic subjects using hypnotic language predicate patterns.

Awareness Predicates

- Accept as true ___
- Aim at ___
- Appreciate ___
- Ascertain ___
- Attend to ___
- Be aware of ___
- Be concerned about ___
- Be conscious of ___
- Be curious about ___
- Be glad about ___
- Be grateful for ___
- Be informed ___

- Be made aware ___
- Be mindful of ___
- Be of the opinion ___
- Be pleased about ___
- Be subjected to ___
- Be told ___
- Bear ___
- Bear in mind ___
- Bear in mind ___
- Become aware of ___
- Believe ___
- Bring to mind ___
- Bring together ___
- Call to mind ___
- Care about ___
- Catch ___
- Center ___
- Chew on ___
- Chew over ___

- Cogitate ___
- Come across ___
- Come across ___
- Come into contact with ___
- Commit to memory ___
- Comprehend ___
- Concentrate on ___
- Consider ___
- Consider it ___
- Contemplate ___
- Converge ___
- Count ___
- Count on ___
- Critically consider ___
- Critically examine ___
- Deem ___
- Deem ___
- Deliberate ___
- Detect ___
- Determine ___
- Dig up ___

- Direct ___
- Discern ___
- Discover ___
- Distinguish ___
- Don't forget ___
- Dredge up ___
- Educe ___
- Encounter ___
- Ensure ___
- Escort ___
- Establish ___
- Evoke ___
- Examine ___
- Experience ___
- Face ___
- Face the facts ___
- Feel ___
- Feel in your bones ___
- Feel in your heart ___
- Find ___
- Find out ___
- Fix ___
- Fixate ___
- Focus on ___
- Gather ___
- Get ___
- Get the impression ___
- Get to know ___
- Get wind of ___
- Go through ___
- Grasp ___
- Guess ___
- Guess what ___
- Hark back to ___
- Harken ___
- Have a feeling ___
- Have down pat ___
- Have off pat ___
- Have the sense of ___
- Hear ___
- Heed ___
- Identify ___
- Imagine ___
- Infer ___
- Intuit ___
- Judge ___
- Keep in mind ___
- Know ___
- Learn ___

- Learn by heart ___
- Listen to ___
- Live through ___
- Locate ___
- Make believe ___
- Make out ___
- Meet ___
- Memorize ___
- Mull over ___
- Note ___
- Notice ___
- Observe ___
- Over hear ___
- Pay attention to ___
- Perceive ___
- Perceive sound ___
- Pick-up ___
- Play make be-lieve and ___
- Play pretend and ___
- Play with ___
- Ponder ___
- Preside over ___

- Pretend to ___
- Realize ___
- Really grasp ___
- Recall ___
- Receive ___
- Recognize ___
- Recognize the value of ___
- Recollect ___
- Reflect ___
- Reflect on ___
- Regard as ___
- Remark ___
- Remember ___
- Reminisce ___
- Respect ___
- Retain ___
- Ruminate ___
- See ___
- Sense ___
- Set ___
- Set your sites on ___
- Sight ___
- Sit in judgment ___
- Smell out ___
- Spot ___
- Study ___
- Suffer ___

- Suffer through ___

- Summon up ___

- Summon up ___

- Suspect ___
- Take in ___
- Take into account ___

- Take into consideration ___

- Take notice of ___

- Taste for yourself ___

- Think ___
- Think about ___

- Think about ___
- Think of ___
- Think through ___

- Trust ___
- Try ___
- Tune into ___
- Turn up ___
- Uncover ___
- Undergo ___
- Understand ___
- Unearth ___
- Value ___
- Weigh up ___
- Welcome ___
- Your mind's eye ___

There are many means by which you can modify these predicates, as well—for example, prefixing 'really' or 'truly' or 'very much' can add varying affect to any of these hypnotic predicates. I suspect you're thinking about all these predicates right now, aren't you? Take into consideration the value of focusing your subject's attention where you want it to go. I suspect you're welcoming all the possibilities to communicate more hypnotically, is it not so?

So switching gears here for just a moment refer back to what I earlier brought to your attention when I subtly pointed out how certain interrogatives are associated with each of these predicates. Expanding this for just a moment I want you to sink into your hypnotic mind this idea that various forms of interrogatives carry with them different weighted affects, mentally. Remember, these predicates and hypnotic language is all about the 'experiences' your hypnotic subjects have when introduced to certain specific combinations of words and sentences strategically using these predicates.

Let's learn about some of the variations of these interrogatives and how you might use them hypnotically to give your hypnotic subjects certain emotional influences:

I.   'Where?' refers to a location in space.

II. 'When?' refers to an experience that happened, is happening, or will happen at some point in time.

III. 'How?' refers to the exploration of attributes, qualities, characteristics, or energy that an object or experience possesses; namely, 'how?' refers to a process or step-by-step sequence.

IV. 'Why?' refers to rationalization of an experience. You must be careful using the word why because it has the tendency to cement concretely whatever happens to be the answer.

When you use this word to question someone you are most often putting them on the 'defensive' and whatever their answer becomes they tend not to change that answer. This word cements structures into specific responses regardless of how general the discussion beforehand.

V.   'Whether' implies a binary choice; that is, it works as a connector for a double-bind question (e.g., Whether we go today or tomorrow makes no difference to me, okay?) In this example it is implied that regardless of the answer the desired outcome to 'go someplace' is going to happen, in any event.

VI.   'What?' refers to an object or idea and tends to create choice and opportunities by expanding the mind to more options and considerations.

VII.   'Which?' infers less choice options and requires a specific choice to be made. It contracts the mind associating it on specific objects or ideas to consider.

VIII.   'Who?' directs focus onto people and away from objects or ideas.

IX.   'Whom?' directs focus onto a specific person; rather than a possible group of people. This form of who is a rarer form, less often used colloquially. It tends to be more passive when used.

X. 'By which means?' This is combination form variation of 'how' and 'what' that tends to get an indirect nominalization as an answer from your hypnotic subject—for example: Question: "By which means will you take the job offer?" Answer: "When I get a knowing it's the right one." Notice how 'knowing' is used as an indirect nominalization.

XI. 'In what way?' This is a variation of 'how' that drives home a more specific answer, most often. Asking 'how' can get you a more generalized response; yet, asking 'In what way' will tend to get you a much less general answer.

XII. 'So what?' Asking 'So what?' tends to revert attention back onto the consequences or deeper meaning of an experience by more rationally exploring and uncovering possible negative belief structures and unsatisfied objections. Be careful using this construction, because it will likely put the persuader on the defensive causing them to cite more directly and aggressively the consequences which will likely occur if you don't follow through with their recommendation, i.e. suggestion.

XIII.   'For what purpose?' This question is usually a better alternative to asking 'why?', because it explores motivation and your hypnotic subject's intentions to be able to more covertly uncover what's behind their behavior. By asking this instead of 'why' you're usually in a better position to leverage change, because remember that 'why' cements responses and you hypnotic subject will refuse in most cases to come off their original answer. For example if you ask: "Why don't you want to buy my product?" and the answer comes back as: "I told you I don't want it!" then chances are you'll lose the sale. However, if you ask: "For what purpose don't you think you want my product?" the answer you get may well likely be: "Well, I just bought a similar one, and it's working just fine, so I don't figure I need another one." The second answer opens up the conversation to exploring the differences between the aspects and functions of the competitor's product and your product, giving an opportunity for the sale to happen.

XIV.   "By what means?" This is another variation of 'how' that tends to clarify intention and chunk down abstraction into something more meaningful and specific.

XV. 'By what method?' This is another variation of 'how' which explores the sequences of an action that led or will likely lead to an end result. This is great for clarifying confusing thoughts that the hypnotic subjects cannot so easily make sense of.

XVI. 'Exactly how?' This is another variation of 'how' that focuses on exacting information about a generalized process. This is a 'challenging' form of 'how' that is much more direct and confrontational.

XVII. 'In what manner?' This is another variation of 'how' and is softer, more permissive, and more likely to get a response from someone who tends to be more explicit behaviorally. If someone is paranoid or suspecting that you have ulterior motives for asking such questions, this form may be more useful for building trust and bypassing the critical faculty of your hypnotic subject.

XVIII. 'Just how?' This is another variation of 'how' that tends to open people up to more precisely explain the process or meaning more clearly to you.

XIX.   'How do you mean?' This is another variation of 'how' and tends to open people up to answering with more intense elucidations that often illuminate and reinforce the answers they give, helping them to sell themselves on their own answers. It definitely makes the responses more meaningful and emotional—thus hypnotic.

XX.   'At what time?' is a variation of 'when'. But this variation tends to deliver to your more precise answers about when specifically.

XXI.   As soon as ___. This is an answer you might want to answer with when someone asks you a 'when' question and you want to be deliver an ambiguous answer. This can also be used as a cause effect pattern: As soon as we finish, the sooner we can go somewhere special.

There are lots of ways you can explore these hypnotic language predicates and use them to communicate more hypnotically as you do hypnotic storytelling or other indirect conversational hypnosis techniques. The main thing to keep in mind are the general patterns themselves; rather than, focusing on every tiny detail I've presented to you in this chapter. The reason for this is you'll be able to more easily remember variations by keeping in mind the parent predicate forms.

For example you may think of 'where' to think of a special predicate, 'what' to think of a matter predicate, 'how' to think about the quality or energy predicate form, and 'when' to think recall the time predicate form. The next step is to play around and use the language predicate variations in certain contexts—these can simply be 'pretend' examples through which you experience in your own mind where the predicate forms take you in reference to space, time, energy, and matter.

You might, for instance, ask yourself to consider what affect "The train is alongside the track," contrasted with "The train is together with the track," and in playing with these predicates make predictions or forecasts generally about the likely perceptions others will infer and draw from these hypnotic constructions.

A last point to end on is the idea that you can hypnotic predicates to space people out and into a hypnotic oblivion by just contracting and expanding the mind by strategically positioning certain predicate forms alongside other opposing forms. For example: "After you hypnotically get less from these patterns you'll actually be getting just more. Notice how 'just' is used to contract the mind, whereas 'more' is used to expand the mind. You can also incorporate negation with these predicates to take the hypnotized mind to places it was not; explicitly, so the mind will open up to new ideas, stepping outside of old belief patterns, into new hypnotic realities, altogether different than what's not known yet. By studying these hypnotic predicate patterns you'll grab hold of a rare form of mastery when it comes to relaying any hypnotic story, anywhere you happen to be, anytime. Yet, and keep this in mind now, but, to the extent you use these hypnotic predicate patterns all the time, is the extent you become a master hypnotic storyteller—astonishing, is it not?

The Recap

Hypnotic storytelling definitely takes time to master. This chapter fills in the mystery constructions that comprise a reality most people 'believe' is actually 'real'. The truth is, reality is plastic; that is, it's a perceptual reality people try but fail to conceptualize.

Language is one of the attributes that make a human being a human being. Language comes from the cortex part of the brain, a new part of the brain responsible for logic, reason, structure, and systematic processing. This is one reason we can write down instructions and then follow them out step-by-step in an exact sequence. Storytelling, though it doesn't have to be rigidly defined as so, is also a structured form; yet, not a formula. There is no, per so, 'wrong' or 'right' way to tell a hypnotic story, as its more a matter of experience and where you are likely to send your hypnotic subject mentally.

The hypnotic story takes on an attribute of 'realness' meaning people become focused and absorbed into the hypnotic stories we tell to the extent that the reality we are creating with our language predicates is forming new realities, places, times, sensations, feelings, and an awareness of objects in reference to other objects, and so on.

The point is that to the point you master being able to use the hypnotic language predicates I've presented you with in this chapter, and more you will no less discover as a result of telling your own unique hypnotic stories, you'll becoming better and better and more skilled as a covert hypnotic storyteller. As soon as you realize your abilities to hypnotize your subjects using hypnotic predicates strategically, learnt from playing around with them experientially, the sooner you'll travel to places yourself beyond where you haven't yet not been. After this happens, everything drops back behind you as if it never stood in your way, and this is a really empowering space you give yourself to be in, now, would you say? Just imagine that.

The awareness predicates take you directly to places the hypnotic storyteller wants you to traverse mentally. Pretend that you have this power inside you to affect changes in others that serve them better than before? Imagine the goodwill it will create between you and them? Really consider these awareness patterns and how they focus your attention on hypnotic storytelling. I know you're in a place somewhere where you're not yet cognitively, and that's okay to a point, because you'll now find yourself realizing things you haven't not realized intuitively already. You know I'm right, right?

The Next Step

Academically, I can tell you the step-by-step logic of the psychological principles applied to hypnotic storytelling; however, I know it wouldn't make you a better hypnotic storyteller.

As I've mentioned I believe that learning comes by doing, and testing for yourself the lessons in this book. I think all learning first happens at the unconscious level, and that the conscious mind takes more time to catch up to what you already have learnt unconsciously, already.

With hypnotic storytelling you have already inside you the knowledge and learnings to be able to capably well tell hypnotic stories. In truth, you already tell hypnotic stories without even being aware when you do.

This book walks you through the process of hypnotic storytelling in a unique way that brings with it clarity. It is better not to overthink hypnotic storytelling, because as soon as you do, you stop being quite so hypnotic.

These exercises will help prepare you to tell hypnotic stories without your critical thinking getting in the way. The 'hypnotic mind' is the 'other mind' which has already learnt the Hypnotic Hero's Journey Model, and now the hypnotic language predicates that linguistically and affectively construct hypnotic realities from the hypnotic stories you tell using them, that I've presented to you. I ask you to suspend your disbelief and trust in the process, and let your stories hypnotize your subjects naturally. Play pretend with these various predicate forms to discover in your own mind experientially where your mind travels. Consider this blind faith in your 'hypnotic mind' comparable to riding a bicycle you've already learned to ride. You might at any moment mount a bicycle in the future and ride it without your conscious mind's interference—brilliantly! In the same way, think about now using these hypnotic predicates to do the same and increase the articulacy and persuasiveness your stories take on.

Have a think about that as you become astonished by your 'hypnotic mind's' ability to affect real change in others—gaining you what you want.

I.   Purchase some 3x5 index cards and everyday write one hypnotic language predicate pattern down from each of the five predicate categories. Then practice using each of the predicates as you go about your day communicating with others and yourself. Be mindful of predicates you've used any time before each new day's patterns, and keep practicing, so you'll keep remembering. Remember, repetition is essential to bringing forward what you already have learnt in your hypnotic mind, so that you also know it consciously. So keep repeating these predicates until they become second-nature for you and also consciously remembered.

II.   Create a very short story, writing it down on paper. After you have finished, write the same story out again, consciously, but switching out the hypnotic reality creation predicates, for the purpose of exploring where various predicates take you mentally. Continue this as often as you like to turn your original hypnotic story into a multitude of hypnotic story variations that can be used in a number of different contexts.

III.   Practice focusing the 'awareness' of the people you encounter using various forms of the 'awareness predicates' and notice the non-verbal and verbal responses you receive. Make mental notes about each pattern and form judgments about the best types of contexts to use the various forms. Once you direct attention, practice shifting awareness using the other hypnotic reality creation predicates.

CHAPTER 4

HYPNOTIC STORYTELLING USING NESTED LOOP SEQUENCES

ero times in my life have I gained as many seemingly random insights as I have when I was hypnotized; namely, when I became hypnotized while reading a hypnotic story that took me to places I wanted to be; yet, had never been before.

I was working on the last chapter of this book earlier today, and I took a break, as I do, to visit the refrigerator. Low and behold, to my astonishment, I saw where Jennifer had brought me some type of Indian vegetarian dish. Indian food is my favorite.

Jennifer is a cool cat. She's my partner in crime. I love her more than I can express with words.

Speaking of cats, I have this cat named Pavlov—I know, paradoxical, right?! Anyway, he has an affinity for hiding in the windowsill that is just above my desk. What he does is jump up on my desk, always when I'm in the thicket of writing something I must get down immediately. He's funny like that, but personality wise he's content to visit with me in between naps to practice his kitty cat communication skills.

Then Mr. Pavlov's goes back to napping, or he entertains himself by provoking our Australian Cattle Dog named Foxy Brown, to herd him around the house. Foxy is young for it, as Mr. Pavlovs keeps her active and her mind alert. Australian Cattle dogs are known for their herding instinct. It's clearly evident to both me and Jennifer, and we find it humorous watching them play together.

With Jennifer I find myself being myself completely. She's the perfect life companion, because she really does love me for me, and not for any other reason. It is an honor for me to reciprocate the same back on her.

As I was finishing up the Indian food, Jennifer walks in from being gone, and tells me she almost picked me up some rice just moments earlier from the Vietnamese restaurant up the street she stopped in to eat at. She told me, "I was going to get your rice, but I had this sense that you'd have eaten the Indian food, by the time I returned, and then the rice would go uneaten, and would go to waste—so I didn't!" I smiled at her, communicating without words how right she'd been to intuit such a thing. Then we turned the conversation off, and I went back to work on this book—inspired to write. Life sure is random, wouldn't you agree?

This randomness can be hypnotic. As I say, being in this state of hypnosis I find myself frequently getting insights that I have no idea where they even come from. Well, maybe that's a lie, as I know they come from my 'hypnotic mind' or what I like to call my 'other mind'. The other mind is a vast storehouse of ambiguous abstractions that are the fragments that show up in our dreams when we go off to sleep at night, soundly.

Not always do we remember our dreams, given the unconscious state that seems to evaporate upon waking in the morning. Under the spell of hypnosis I find that these incredible insights seem to come to me and be retained without forgetting them. I keep a writer's journal for noting these inspirational idea that I'll likely, as has been the pattern in the past, use in later works I write.

This chapter is on hypnotic storytelling using covert nested loop sequences to chain stories together in such a way that it opens Pandora's Box in the sense that you'll have be free to unleash and implement so many layers of hypnotic techniques that straightaway your hypnotic subject will be dropped into the hypnotic state allowing you to change minds, create new belief patterns in their minds, and even covertly embed post hypnotic directives that will have a high rate of success being carried out. This is a method for telling hypnotic stories that utilizes the psychological principle known as the Zeirgarnik Effect. By applying this hypnotic storytelling model you'll wet your subject's appetites and have them hanging on every hypnotic word you speak, I promise you. These types of hypnotic stories are insatiable; that is to say, your hypnotic subjects won't be able to get enough of your hypnotic stories and in some instances I've even experienced some of my hypnotic subjects stomping down a path to my doorway just to get me to finish a story or tell them another. Be forewarned that this method is highly hypnotic and extremely powerful for creating new persuasions in people's minds.

Why are Nested Loop Sequences Effective?

You have to understand the psychology behind utilizing this nested loop sequence approach. Firstly, stories are told all the time, and without our even being aware we're telling them. Hypnotic storytelling itself is a hypnotic process that naturally happens, because we're hypnotized by our thoughts most of the time; namely, when we tell our hypnotic stories, anyhow, but consciously.

I mean, stop what you're doing for just a moment, and really consider what I'm about to have you seriously consider, here. I want you to put your full attention on this—it's very important!...

You see, we've all found ourselves in a conversation with someone exchanging stories back and forth. Stories are great for building rapport with perfect strangers; viz., one reason sales professionals engage their potential customers with random stories. It builds trust.

When we listen to someone else tell us a story it sometimes triggers a memory or an idea in our minds that, next thing we know, we're telling them a story too. Sometimes we are interrupted by other people in the middle of telling a story for them to cut-in and tell us a mini-story they simply must get out before they forget.

There's an etiquette that is observed naturally, at least for most of us, that simply state is: (a) don't interrupt me until I finish my story, and (b) if I tell you a story, I'm compelled, or expected to reciprocate and listen to your story back. Of course, and everybody knows this, this etiquette is an unspoken rule of thumb, but one that often gets broken. Some people will spout off a number of stories and then for whatever reason excuse themselves from the conversation citing a logically rational reason why they need to go. Most people simply let them escape, though some people will harbor a judgment, but mostly we think nothing of it and go about our day when it happens to us.

When we watch commercials on television, between segments of a program we're engaged in, many of these television commercials are mini-stories that get weaved between the main programming. Some of these commercials have a 'to be continued' ending, which implies that we'll have to keep watching the commercials in the future to find out what happens next. Some programs in fact do this.

I remember when I was a child sitting in front of the television watching a program named, "Matlock". Many of the episodes were suspended until the following week when the program would air again. All throughout the week I would wonder what the ending would be. I also had to make darn-sure I didn't miss the next episode for any reason; elsewise, I would never learn the ending. Psychologically this affect is known as the Zeirgarnik Effect. Let me explain this to you.

The Zeirgarnik Effect

Bluma Wulfovna Zeirgarnik was a Russian psychologist who did research which turned up that results which support that individuals who are interrupted while engaged in a task are much more likely to remember the task, than had they not been interrupted.

This research extended her professor Kurt Lewin's Field Research Theory that details how a task, once begun, brings with it a task-specific tension. Lewin pointed out to Zeirgarnik one day during lunch his observation that the waiter was able to recall meal tickets which were not yet paid, far better than meal tickets in which the customers had already paid this bill.

The Zeirgarnik Effect is this phenomenon that happens when a task goes uncompleted, once interrupted. There is a discomfort and tension that results when something has been interrupted, halting the progress of the task's completion.

Furthermore, when a task is interrupted, not allowed to be finished, there is a psychological tendency that naturally occurs which causes the subject to recall remembering the uncompleted task far better than other similar completed tasks.

In What Way Does the Zeirgarnik Effect Play a Role in Hypnotic Storytelling; Specifically, When Utilizing Nested Loop Sequences?

Now that you understand the Zeirgarnik Effect, let's explore for a moment how this psychological effect is applied to hypnotic storytelling; namely, the nested loop sequences. Firstly, understand that when we tell a story, and break it, meaning that we stop the story to tell another story; that is to say, leaving it 'uncompleted' as well as 'interrupted' the Zeirgarnik Effect is fundamentally being applied to the essence of the hypnotic story. When this occurs, an amnesia happens causing the hypnotic subject to mentally still be focused on the interrupted story that was broke, and not so focused on the new story being told.

In Zeirgarnik's research often was the case that when a task was interrupted intentionally, yet covertly, the subject became rather hostile, only wanting to complete the first task, before going on to the next task. People want closure and finality when it comes to tasks. It is the same when it comes to hearing a hypnotic story: people want to hear the end of one story, before they start hearing the next story.

In my mind, this may be due to the conditioning of society telling us that we should set goals and make lists and not go on to the next objective, before completing the objective we're working on now.

When someone is completely focused on one story it has control over their attention and awareness. Being confronted back-to-back with a completely different hypnotic story, the subject is defocused on it, because they're

so intensely focused on the one preceding it. This in return causes a hypnotic trance to result. When the subject
becomes more and more hypnotized, as more new stories
are told, and broken; left unfinished, the subject can then
be fed covert post-hypnotic suggestions which are quite
likely to be carried out afterwards.

What are Nested Loop Sequences?

Nested loop sequences are fundamentally hypnotic stories,
which are told, one after another, in a sequence, but,
which have intentionally been interrupted about 2/3 of
the way through the story, just before the height of the
climax, and left incomplete; that is to say, none of the hypnotic stories have been allowed to finish being told.

When you get to the last story you wish to tell, you
finish it without interruption, and then, backtracking, revisit the story told just before it, which wasn't finished,
and then finish it. Then you revisit the story told just before that story, and finish it. You are essentially completing the loop of each story which came before the next in
reverse order, until you complete the circle and find yourself finishing the first story you originally began telling.
This is the nested loop sequence.

This hypnotic storytelling model is quite covert and indirect; namely, because we do this all the time, naturally,
when telling stories. Sometimes someone will begin telling a story and their phone will ring, and they'll start to
tell the person on the other end of the phone a completely

different story, unrelated to the story they were telling the person standing right in front of them. The person over-hearing this new story, may be half-interested because they're still mentally caught-up in the original story that has been interrupted. This person may take on feelings that harbor anger towards you or the person calling you, because they find it rude that you'd stop to take a phone call; however, I'm going to suggest that they're also experiencing the Zeirgarnik Effect in action, whereby they're experiencing the task-specific tension of not having closure on the story they were listening to you tell.

This tension, and their desire for you to finish your story may become even more increased should you have to run, without being able to finish the story. Theoretically speaking, this stress will not diminish ever, until your hypnotic subject get closure and you finish telling them the story. Also, true, is that they'll not forget the story until it is finished being told.

How to Make Your Hypnotic Storytelling More Hypnotically Affective Using Nested Loop Sequences?

Exactly how you make your hypnotic stories more hyp-notic is up to you; yet, this section will walk you through some proven strategies you can immediately use to make your already spellbinding stories, even more hypnotizing.

To start, I want you to take a revisit to the start of this chapter. You see, I told you a series of stories: (a) *Me Writing This Book*, (b) *Break to the Refrigerator for Indian Food*, (c) *Jennifer My Partner in Crime*, and (d) *My Cat Mr. Pavlov*.

Take a good look over these stories. They aren't really laden with hypnotic language, and my intention was you'd overlook them without much thought. I wanted them to be a covert example used to teach you how to structure your stories using the nested loop sequencing technique.

The first story is one about me writing this book. It's nothing out of the ordinary. For this reason it doesn't trigger your critical faculty to raise a suspicion, merely because it congruent with the purpose of this book—it fits the context. The next story is a soft break, though a bit random, as I'm taking a break from the first story; telling you, or rather giving you clues into my writing process. It flows naturally from the first story; thus, we call this a soft break. A soft-break is where we transition from telling one story into the next by making a smooth (soft) transition. The next story is a hard-break; namely, because I'm transitioning into a completely different story, i.e. one about my love-life, which doesn't have anything to do really with writing this book or my writing process. The next story is yet another hard break because I'm now transitioning into a story about my cat.

The story I share about Mr. Pavlov, my cat, is the last story I told. For this reason I completed it, without a break. After completing this story, notice how I then went back to the story I told previous to it; that is, the story named, *Jennifer My Partner in Crime*. I complete this story.

Then I jump back up to the story I titled: *Break to the Refrigerator for Indian Food*. I finish it. Then I transition back in, nice and seamlessly, to the story: *Me Writing This Book*.

The way I've done is apply the nested loop sequence. Now consider what would happen if I stopped this book here, without writing another word. Would you feel cheated? Would you feel a type of tension or discord building inside you? Maybe, you're beginning to wonder if I'd really do such a thing? Maybe you're actually feeling the feelings you'd have felt, had I stopped this book in its tracks, here, now.

This experience you're experiencing is psychological, and backed by scientific research. Please, don't take tension; I'm not about to cheat you out of these lessons in covert indirect hypnotic storytelling. You can trust I'll give you more value than you expect! I promise you!

Let's learn some more about this process, shall we?

The Nested Loop Sequence

The nested loop sequence is a very powerful hypnotic storytelling technique. I mentioned to you before about how hypnotic amnesia is caused when a random break in one story happens, and another begins. Another point I want to bring to your attention is how this nested loop sequencing also has the ability to employ hypnotic fractionation.

Fractionation is a powerful hypnotic deepening technique. It literally is when you hypnotize someone and then abruptly bring them out of trance, and right then abruptly drop them back into hypnosis again. Then you repeat this process over and over again until your hypnotic subject is deeply mesmerized.

You see, each time you fractionate; that is, drop them back into hypnosis after taking them out of hypnosis, the subject goes even deeper into hypnosis than they were previously.

Think about it this way to better get an idea of the experience the subject is experiencing when you apply fractionation: Imagine taking a long trip in your car, and you're the driver. Your partner in crime or some friend is sitting beside you in the passenger seat. For a period of time you both remain talk-less. The long stretch of highway in front of you creates what is called Highway Hypnosis. You begin to zone out. You're now not really paying attention to anything in particular. Your self-talk has quieted. You're now simply a tool in the hands of the universe acting to get your car from point *a* to point *b*. All of a sudden, unexpectedly, your friend touches your shoulder and says, "Are you awake?" Instantly, you become conscious, out of trance, and begin paying attention to what's going on around you. You assure your friend you're awake and fully paying attention to everything going on. You then start a conversation that keeps your focus for a while. Then another bout of silence happens. Again you're hypnotized to the road again. This time you really trance out, deeper than before. At some point, your friend, who's been quiet, bursts out laughing hysterically from something they've been reading in a book. This instantly brings you back to where you were in consciousness and you inquire about what's so funny. Your friend tells you and then goes back to reading their book. Once more you drop back into a trance. Only this time you're really feeling the effect of a very deep hypnosis; having driven for so long, and having been up and down in your consciousness and unconsciousness that you're in an even deeper trance. This same process happens over and over again, until eventually, you sense it's unsafe for you to be driving, so you pull off on some exit ramp, using the excuse that you need to get gas, use the restroom, and get something in your stomach. You need to reorient and recondition yourself to consciousness so that you can safely get back on the road and get to where you want to be.

Another example, to give you the experience of hypnotic fractionation, occurs when you're in high school and sitting through your first class. You're still not quite awake, having been awaken by your mother or father way too early in the morning and told it's time to get ready for school. Now you're doing your best to stay awake, and just about the time you're nice and zoned out, deep under the spell of hypnosis, the bell rings, alerting you this class is over and it's time to get to the next. During the next class you are now once again alert, having stretched your legs, refocused your attention away from that boring class, and now sitting in a completely different classroom. After some time what happens? That's right. You are about 2/3 the way through this class and once more you're under the spell of hypnosis—only deeper hypnotized. Now, just about to fall asleep on your desk, you hear the bell ring a screaming sound that has you thanking some higher power that this class is over. You repeat this process, and when you get to the end of your day arriving home, your parent asks you: "How was your day today?" In the back of your mind you think: "This day has moved forward faster than I could keep up." What you actually say though is: "Just another day in paradise!" You then get fractionated again when you start doing your homework, then stop for dinner, then start again, formerly stop for a snack, then start again, then stop to watch a program or two on television, then start again, then stop to talk on the phone with a classmate, then start again, then stop to call it a night—you're exhausted and will be asleep the minute your head touches your pillow; however, you'll experience this hypnotic fractionation all over again before you know it when you're awaken to another day of the same hypnotic experience.

So I hope I've painted a good picture in your mind of what the experience of hypnotic fractionation does in terms of deepening the hypnotic experience. Throughout our waking day, we experience waking hypnosis, which occurs naturally about ever 90 – 120 minutes of our day, in which we zone out, daydream, and for lack of a better word become 'hypnotized'. These naturally occurring hypnotic cycles are known as 'circadian rhythms'. They're as natural as the 24 hour sleep cycles that happen to you, or the monthly menstruation cycles that occur in women, or the seasonal depression cycles that happen year to year. These happen without us thinking much about them.

Back to hypnotic storytelling and in particular as are told using the hypnotic nested loop sequences to deepen hypnosis using the fractionation that happens when someone listening becomes emotionally involved and captivated in one story, only to be unexpectedly and abruptly interrupted with another completely different story. The new story takes them out of the previous story, reawakening them to consciousness, and after some time passes, and they calibrate to the new story being told, dropping into an even deeper hypnosis, by the time you finish your storytelling you can be rest assured that your hypnotic subject will be very much a walking zombie likely to do whatever you want them to.

I may be dramatizing the affect using a metaphoric zombie analogy, but I'm probably not too far off base. In fact when someone joins a cult, one of the first things the cult may do is create a type of hypnosis brought on by sleep deprivation. I've seen this happen first hand. When the hypnotic subject, i.e. new cult member starts to go without much if any sleep, for an extended period of time, they start to lose their identity and sense of self, and begin taking on the characteristics of a mind-controlled zombie, who will do whatever is asked of them.

Hypnotic storytelling is used a lot in mind-control cults. The stories may at first seem preposterous and unbelievable entirely; however, it is fascinating to observe the transformation of someone sleep deprived and inundated with the cult ideology become indoctrinated so quickly and easily without warning.

Now that you have a general idea about the hypnotic affect brought about by using nested loop sequences, here's the process outlined for you step-by-step which will assist you learning the nested loop sequencing pattern:

I.   Step 1: Tell your first story, but break it about two-thirds of the way through the story, right before the peak of the climax. You can use either a hard break; namely, one which you abruptly switch to telling an altogether different story, or you can use a soft break; namely where you'll slowly transition seamlessly from one hypnotic story into the next, without your hypnotic subject realizing that one story has been stopped and another begun. By the way, a soft break can create a nice hypnotic confusion that can also deepen the hypnotic experience.

II.   Step 2: Tell your next story, again breaking two-thirds of the way through, right before the peak of the climax.

III.   Step 3: Continue telling your hypnotic stories, breaking two-thirds of the way through, like before. Note: I've found it best to use between five and twelve stories when utilizing this technique.

IV.   Step 4: When you get to the last hypnotic story you're going to tell, instead of breaking, finish the story completely.

V.   Step 5: After your last story is finished, revisit the story told just before it, and complete that hypnotic story.

VI.   Step 6: Continue finished each preceding story that was told before the one you've just finished until you have completed the circle finishing the first hypnotic story you told.

So now you have the basic hypnotic nested loop sequence that you can model yourself, to tell deeply hypnotic stories. This approach does take some time to master. I find my students have an easier go mastering it when they stop to think how they naturally tell stories in this fashion all the time without consciously being aware of it. I mean, we all interrupt our own stories to tell another story about something else that's either happened to us, or to someone we know, and in the process leave a lot of stories incomplete. Then what follows is you'll run into someone sometime down the road and they'll ask you about a story you started telling them, but forgot to finish. This is the power of this approach! You know when someone hasn't forgotten a story you were in the middle of sharing, but which for whatever reason couldn't finish, that you're more hypnotic a storyteller than you even realize.

I wanted to also note that people are naturally conditioned to want to be hypnotized or not. There is a time and place for hypnosis. When we're working and need to focus on what it is we're doing, and there's pressure to stay alert and at our best consciously, well then we prefer to take measures to stay alert. These energy drinks, pills, etc. are used by millions of people, for this reason. However, likewise, there's a time to mellow out, perhaps after working a long hard day doing something that took a lot of our mental power or physical stamina, or perhaps when we just feel like we need to disconnect from reality and meditate or do something quiet, like for instance yoga, or praying, etc. These types of activities are my hypnosis inducing. People listen to music while sitting by themselves to unwind and get inside their head and think things out. People take walks or run to collect their thoughts and again these are hypnotic inducing activities. So there's the tendency to want to be hypnotized, just like there's the tendency to want to be completely conscious and focused on what we're doing.

I tell you this, because it is important to understand the nature of hypnosis and why people use hypnosis, what it is, and how we as hypnotists can actually borrow naturally occurring hypnotic states or self-induced hypnotic states to achieve our ends.

We go to college to learn how to critically think and be alert to details that demand our scrutiny. One way of looking at this is to understand that school is used to help us 'not' be hypnotized. You see, most people tend to think that hypnosis is something that is intentionally done to them; however, what most people fail to realize is we're more hypnotized than we're not, and so the thing being intentionally done to us is training in 'not' being hypnotized. Most people are backward in their thinking when it comes to hypnosis versus non-hypnosis.

What if You Use Hypnotic Nested Loops In Other Sequences?

In this chapter I taught you the 'basic' hypnotic nested loop structure. Now, let's play some, and learn how else we might use nested loops, but in different sequences.

You can actually embed nested loops inside of other nested loops, which will give you an even greater hypnotic affect. You can do this starting as you would, but after telling a few stories, complete the last one and then revisit the one above it, and then begin telling another completely different story, breaking it 2/3 through, and then telling another and another, and eventually, when you've finished your last story, complete it entirely, and then retrace your steps, but skip the forth story that you already completed, and instead finish story three, two, and of course your original first story.

You can actually make it a game; that is, these nested loop sequences. The more you practice playing around with various nested loop combination the more natural telling hypnotic stories in this way will be for you. The sooner you become accustomed to telling multiple hypnotic stories in this way the sooner you'll reach mastery of hypnotic storytelling.

You'll be astonished to discover you already hypnotically know how to tell hypnotic stories using this method, when you consciously catch yourself telling stories in this fashion. One way of consciously catching yourself telling a truly powerful hypnotic story is to watch the body language and non-verbal cues of your hypnotic subject.

It's easy to observe your hypnotic subject trancing out and going into deeper and deeper states of hypnosis. All you have to do is watch for their pupils to dilate. A dilated pupil is an expanded pupil. Some people call it 'wide-eyed', which I think is ironic, given that the expression 'wide-eyed and bushy-tailed' usually denotes someone freshly alert and not hypnotized. Semantics, right?!!

You'll also tell when someone is hypnotized by their body language; namely, because it will be slowed down. Also, their facial muscles will relax and soften up and sink somewhat. Their mind will not be as alert. They'll tend to look zoned-out, and zombie-looking. Trust me, you'll know when someone is hypnotized. If you just pay attention in fact to people, which is a good habit to get in, you'll see people all the time entering the hypnotic state.

The Recap

In this chapter I taught you the psychological principle of the Zeirgarnik Effect, and how it creates a hypnotic state, yet also how it creates hypnotic amnesia, as well as a staunch memory and focus on unfinished hypnotic stories you deliver to your hypnotic subjects. I also taught you about the hypnotic nested loop sequence technique for making your hypnotic stories even more potent to the extent your hypnotic subjects will be hanging on every word you speak. We also looked at other possibilities you can play around with and experiment with by considering other possible sequences for embedding nested loops inside of other nested loops. Lastly we touched on the nature of hypnosis and how most people are backwards in their thinking of hypnosis; thinking hypnosis is something done to someone, when in fact most people are hypnotized more often than they think.

The Next Step

Academically, I can tell you the step-by-step logic of the psychological principles applied to hypnotic storytelling; namely, as it relates to the Nested Loop Sequences. However, I know it wouldn't make you a better hypnotic storyteller, just more knowledgeable on this subject matter.

As I've mentioned I believe that learning comes by doing, and testing for yourself the lessons in this book. I think all learning first happens at the unconscious level, and that the conscious mind takes more time to catch up to what you already have learnt unconsciously, already.

With hypnotic storytelling you have already inside you the knowledge and learnings to be able to capably well tell hypnotic stories. In truth, you already tell hypnotic stories without even being aware when you do.

This book walks you through the process of hypnotic storytelling in a unique way that brings with it clarity. It is better not to overthink Hypnotic Storytelling, the Zeirgarnik Effect, or Nested Loop Sequences, because as soon as you do, you stop being quite so hypnotic.

These exercises will help prepare you to tell hypnotic stories without your critical thinking getting in the way. The 'hypnotic mind' is the 'other mind' which has already learnt the Hypnotic Hero's Journey Model, the Hypnotic

Language Predicates that linguistically and affectively construct hypnotic realities from the hypnotic stories you tell using them, that I've presented to you, and now even the Zeirgarnik Effect, Hypnotic Nested Loop Sequences, and Hypnotic Fractionation that can be implemented into your hypnotic stories. I ask you to suspend your disbelief and trust in the process, and let your stories hypnotize your subjects naturally. Play with using the hypnotic nested loop hypnotic storytelling method to be able to discover in your own mind experientially where your mind travels, and how your subject's react to your hypnotic stories. Consider this blind faith in your 'hypnotic mind' comparable to riding a bicycle you've already learned to ride. You might at any moment mount a bicycle in the future and ride it without your conscious mind's interference—astonishingly! In the same way, think about now using these nested loop sequences to do the same and position yourself as an amazingly terrific hypnotic storyteller.

Have a think about that as you become astounded by your 'hypnotic mind's' ability to affect real change in others—gaining you what you want.

I.   Invent five hypnotic stories and map out where the break should be in each story. This is usually about two-thirds of the way through the story and just before the climax peaks. Then create the basic hypnotic nested loop structure. Memorize these stories perfectly and share the stories with others in sequence and simply watch the hypnotic effect that happens to come over your subjects.

II.   Devise a powerfully intriguing story using the Hypnotic Hero's Journey model. This story should be able to captivate your hypnotic subject's focus immediately and keep it glued there in the story. Just before the climax, roughly two-thirds of the way through, break the story with some excuse and leave your hypnotic subject to wonder what the ending is. Observe how quickly it takes them to approach you about the story's ending.

III. Go out and tell hypnotic stories using the hypnotic nested loop sequence, but without thinking about too much. Observe yourself consciously unconsciously telling hypnotic stories without your critical mind stepping in to hinder your abilities to tell hypnotic stories using this approach. Practice on several people covertly and simply observe the result.

CHAPTER 5

HYPNOTIC LANGUAGE PATTERNS

Briefly we've gone over hypnotic language predicates that create plastic realities in the minds of your hypnotic subjects. Now we learn about true hypnotic language mastery which will supercharge your hypnotic stories to make them even more hypnotic than you might ever imagine.

In this chapter I'll take you through two hypnosis linguistic models which were modeled using NLP modeling techniques. These two hypnotic language models were constructed around the artfully vague hypnotic language patters of Milton Erickson, as well as the direct language patterns of other effective psychotherapists. The two models I'm referring to are the Milton Model and the Meta Model.

Now, to be fair to the reader, I have previously written about these two models in other books, and have borrowed much of the exact content in this chapter from other publications of mine. Even so, I have adapted this chapter around the application of these language patterns for explicit using them in hypnotic storytelling.

THE MILTON MODEL

There are two models I'll be teaching you in this chapter. The first is the Milton Model. This is the hypnotic language you'll be using to hypnotize people while delivering your hypnotic stories. The Milton Model is used to speak artfully vague in a way that allows you to generalize, delete, and distort language for the same of being indirectly implicit in your communication with others. This is what is referred to in Ericksonian schools of hypnosis as 'Indirect Hypnosis'. The artfully vague language patterns of Milton Hyland Erickson were modeled by Dr. Richard Bandler and Dr. John Grinder, the founders of Neuro-Linguistic Programming. What we have as the Milton Model is derived from their work modeling him. Since the 1970s when this model came about the language patterns have been tested time and time again to prove their efficacy hypnotizing people conversationally. I can tell you with absolute surety they work astonishingly well in the context of hypnotic storytelling.

This particular model utilizes patterns that are used in everyday conversations all the time that do three things well; namely: 'distort', 'delete', and 'generalize' meanings conveyed by message delivers to message receiver.

The way these language patterns work is to make someone believe that an idea is actually their idea. The beauty of this model is in how you'll be able to communicate with people on multiple levels. In one light the subject will intuit as a result of your behavior, attitude, and what you express yourself to represent to them, as someone communicating to them directly in a way that they can intuit what you mean, without actually knowing 100% what you're saying. On the other hand while they think they know what you mean you'll actually be secretly communicating something entirely different to their 'other' mind. Because people naturally assume congruence from the people they speak with it is safe to assume people mean one thing when they actually may mean something entirely different. We assume meaning in other words based on our model of the world and the maps we create of reality through our own individual experiences. When someone is apparently sincere, as we believe a sincere person is represented as, in actuality, using these language patterns, the person doing the communicating may be communicating incongruent from what is assumed.

Consciously people think one thing and unconsciously they very well could be perceiving something entirely different—a different message altogether.

The other model I'll be teaching you in this chapter after we cover the Milton Model, is the Meta Model.

The Meta Model is thought by many in the fields of NLP and Hypnosis to be the inverse of the Milton Model. In the Meta Model we're actually using our understanding and knowledge of the Milton Model to challenge people in exactly what it is that they say.

Now this gives us a heavy edge in conversation and communicating with others, because is one sense we can use artfully vague language to persuade, manipulate, coax, conform, and bend peoples' will to whatever we want it to be. We can use Meta Model Violations to challenge someone when they use artfully vague hypnotic language and persuasion patterns on us in the course of natural unconscious communication.

To bring more clarity to what I'm saying, let me just say that the Milton Model is a model that can be used to covertly hypnotize people and have them believe and think and act on what we want them to do. The Meta Model Violations will ensure that other people do not use these same hypnotic language patterns on us to influence us to bend to their will.

We talk in generalities, distort information as we communicate partly what we mean, and delete information as we talk to people leaving it to them to fill in the blanks with what we actually mean.

This particular model, i.e. the Milton Model, is useful for distorting meaning, deleting meaning, and generalizing in a vague enough way to have people assume they know what we're communicating without directly coming out and saying specifically what we mean.

The Meta Model is made up violations that guard and protect against people using language vaguely.

We hear people say such statements like: "You know what I mean." Often times we agree to be agreeable and make our own meaning of what they must mean; viz. assuming we should know, by the way the communicator supposed we should. Nobody wants to be made the fool, do they now?

Really though, the receiver may not honestly know for sure what the person meant by that statement: "You know what I mean." The Meta Model would have us asking: "Mean by what?" to gain greater clarity. I don't know about you, but I don't want to assume I know what someone means when I don't for sure know what they mean. Think how many times you've just gone along with someone for the sake of keeping rapport and wanting to be thought to be on their same wavelength. People do this all the time, so rest assured, you're not alone in this. But, don't ask me who those people are, as I have no idea myself, and neither do you.

Another example might be: "Everybody can learn hypnotic storytelling." This seems reasonable and with a little authority, conviction in my voice, and me looking you straight in the eye, you may likely believe me, because you believe without doubt that I believe this to be a truism. However, Meta Model violations would challenge; having us ask: "Everybody?!!!" (Questioning that 'everybody' alive on the planet is able to learn hypnotic storytelling.)

Asking a challenging question like this would tend to put the message sender on the defensive shaking the foundation of their conviction that everybody can learn something and specifically 'hypnotic storytelling'.

When people are often put on the defensive, because of such a challenge, they start to panic and their critical mind starts to shut down and they tend to go into a trance. Very often looking at them suspiciously, as if to imply they are a liar, will cause them to keep talking, having them continue trying to support the claim they made, or make up some excuse, or even try and rebuild rapport with you, and in the process they start to stumble over their words and their communication falls apart. They hesitate, making them appear and even feel guilty and not so intelligent, and so on. This puts you the challenger in a very powerful position, because now the sender wants only to get back on your good side, so they try relentlessly to rebuild rapport and in the process you achieve the upper hand over them in a negotiation, debate, sell, or persuasion situation.

When we raise doubts surrounding what someone is claiming as true, it is easy to persuade and influence them, because by now they're already going into trance—so you can hypnotize them rather immediately, then, in that very moment.

It is for this reason that I want you to learn both language models; namely, so that you can communicate hypnotically, like Milton Erickson did, but also protect yourself by being able to challenge the credibility of others when they communicate persuasively or hypnotically, and shed doubt on what it is they're claiming to be true, which isn't proven.

Now this may sound elementary to some of you reading this, but I mentioned in the introduction that I have known things unconsciously but always consciously. This is one of those points where most of the literature out there hasn't clarified for people to where they could process it consciously. For this reason, I want you to really get the implication and value from what I'm actually saying.

So let me put it so you can get what I'm saying consciously by telling you a little story.

Years ago I was involved in a research project where I learnt a lot about Hindu politics. I knew a great deal from my research.

During this period I happened to volunteer to pick people up at the Detroit International Airport to take them to a nonprofit event that I was a volunteer at.

One of the guys I picked up was a Harvard professor.

I began an engaging conversation with this man sharing with him my research and understanding about a particular political party. I made a statement which he challenged. The statement I had made was a generalization about a particular aspect of the political party for which I was not educated on.

I had assumed that this man knew nothing on the topic I was discussing, and that was an error on my part.

Instantly I lost face. I knew in that instant that he knew I didn't know what I was talking about, and this instantly discredited me.

Because I felt threatened by this man's intelligence and my lack thereof my amygdala kicked in and I retreated from further arguing my point. I actually, in that moment, slipped into a hypnotic trance.

Another vital point to make mention of is when you challenge someone and they go into a trance you will be able to utilize this to your advantage and implant hypnotic suggestion in their 'other' mind; however, the codicil here is to let you know that people tend to only want to associate themselves with people whom they perceive are either on their level of authority or else beneath their level. You'll break rapport with someone most often if they perceive you as having more authority than them. You'll be perceived as a threat to them; like this man was to me.

The point I want to drive home to you is that when you challenge someone and they perceive you as having more authority than you most often what happens is they will go into a trancelike state, i.e. hypnosis, to where you'll be able to communicate with them hypnotically and implant seeds of suggestion in their heads. Only take this approach however if you are okay with them dissociating and retreating from the communication and from you.

So now let's dip our fee in the water and start learning these language patterns so you can communicate hypnotically and have people hanging on every word you say as if they cannot get enough of being around you.

Cause Effect Patterns (Causality)

These are, if you think back to about third grade or third standard, where you were taught in your elementary English class about If/Then statements.

If/then statements are the classic cause effect pattern.

Many might have heard your parents say to you at the dinner table: "If you eat your vegetables, then you can have desert." This very persuasive speak, given a child will assume that they will not be able to have desert until they have eaten their vegetables. Parents have used this and similar cause effect patterns on children to persuade them and control them and their behavior.

Another cause effect pattern I have frequently used in sales calls is: "After you get ___, you know ___." This could, for example, be used to assume a sale. For example: "After you get this ad, you'll know why everybody repurchases from me year after year every year." You see in order to know why everybody repurchases, they have first advertise. If they don't advertise, then they don't get to eat their desert; that is, in this case, know why everybody repurchases the ad. See how hypnotic this pattern is and how well it affects people mentally to where they out of shear curiosity will make the purchase, because they get to a point where they simply 'must' know why everybody repurchases. There must, in their mind, be a logical explanation, for which you can be sure they're imagining already, just after you've said a statement like this one. So cause effect patterns are highly persuasive and hypnotic.

Nominalization Patterns

Now nominalizations, these language patterns, these are what happen when we take a verb, adverb, or adjective, and turn them into a noun.

What this does is take an action or the like which is descriptive or fluid or some type of action that is fleeting, and transitions it into something that 'concrete' or 'fixed' or 'static' in how it is perceived. So we take something dynamic and make it cemented. We're taking an action and turning it into a fixed object.

Now why do you think this would be useful?

Think about it like this. Think about these two words: (a) believe, and (b) belief. The first word, i.e. believe, is a verb. The impression people get is that the word 'believe' is less fixed. Now look at the work 'belief' and notice how it is more permanent sounding; that is, almost eternal in a sense. Now let's compare the two for contrast by looking at two sentences using both: (a) "I believe God exists," and (b) "My belief is God exists."

People believe things all the time. The first sentence could be changed next week. It's less permanent; that is to say, less owned by the person. The second sentence the person is taking ownership of something, an object, which is called a 'belief.' It's ownership. There's much more attachment to this ownership of a 'belief' than there is to merely believing in something called a God.

Incidentally, I purposefully used the word God in this example, because God is an abstract noun, which is different from a nominalization. Like a nominalization though you cannot, generally speaking, pick up God and wheel him/her off in a wheelbarrow, any more than you could wheel of a 'belief'. So understand the difference between a nominalization and an abstract noun. The word 'nominalization' itself, ironically, is a nominalization. The verb 'nominalize' has been converted into the noun 'nominalization'.

I think you now <u>understand</u> what I mean by this, because it is easy to get these <u>understandings,</u> is it not? Just like when you <u>learn</u> these <u>learnings</u> you'll have <u>learnt</u> much, right? I wonder if I should tell you that <u>hypnotizing</u> <u>hypnotists</u> can be <u>hypnotizing</u>. You may already have a <u>knowing</u> about what you don't yet <u>know</u>, mightn't you?

When I used to sell advertising for a yellow-pages directory I could have asked the customer: "Do you want to advertise?" or I could have asked: "Do you want to own some fantastic advertising?" One is intangible; the other tangible. People want to experience owning something tangible more so than intangible. When people sell things that are intangible like insurance or advertising nominalizations let you create the experience someone is purchasing something tangible, even though they are not.

When someone tells you that they're depressed what they're actually meaning is that something is depressing them. The very word 'depression' a nominalization is concrete—an obstacle standing in the way of them experiencing happiness. By shifting this to ask a question like: "What is going on in your life at this moment that is depressing you?" you object less owned mentally and more fluid and able to be overcome just as easily as it came to be.

Complex Equivalence Patterns

This pattern is when two things are said to be equal to one another. I want you to think about an 'equals' sign (=). In mathematics whatever is on one side of the equals sign must be equivalent to what is on the other side of the equals sign for the equation to be true.

In our English vocabulary there are words which represent this equals sign; namely: (a) equals, (b) equates to, (c) means, (d) amounts to, (e) makes equal, (f) makes, and (g) totals, and (h) be the same as.

An astonishing thing happens when you use these words to make equal two completely separate and unequal ideas—people, without question, believe you, and agree with you.

Here's an example to illustrate this point: "When people love you, it means they want you to do good in life." Do you believe this statement to be true? Most wouldn't question it, if I spoke it to them, because it is plausible enough most would tend to find it easier to agree and accept what I said was true.

If you examine closely this statement, however, you'll see that what comes before the 'it means' is not in any way equal to what comes after. This statement is a lie, unless you find yourself still believing it. It is possible to love someone, many might claim, and still wish, out of jealousy, secretly hope you'll fall on your face and fail. I have a friend who calls these friends 'haters'. I'm still not sure what she exactly means by this term.

Studying these language is the same as studying anything else—you have to practice them to get good at them. This statement I just started this new paragraph with is yet another example of a complex equivalence. The statement is plausible enough you likely went along with it, but, and truthfully speaking, it isn't true. You see, not all studying is the same, not all studying lead to the same result, nor does everything require practice for you to master learning it. Some things are difficult to study for, while others are easier. Again, you see, now, why this persuasion is actually false.

Universal Quantifier Patterns

These language patterns are generalizations that universally claim to quantify something as true for everybody. These words are words like: (a) all, (b) every, (c) each, (d) nobody, (e) everybody, (f) none, (g) never, and (h) always. Other universal quantifiers are: (a) certainly, (b) forever, (c) absolutely, etc.

Everyone loves money. This statement is most likely false. All it takes is one person to say they don't love money, for it to be disproven. Even so, if you couldn't find anyone to disagree with this statement, it is still one that can easily be discredited and doubted as true because it is impossible to most likely to ask 'everybody' everywhere if they love money or not.

This being said, many people will believe and take what you say when you use universal quantifiers to be the truth and not question your authority.

If you use these universal quantifier patterns abstractly enough in your communications with others you'll find those people you're communicating with will start to become hypnotized—for example, "Everybody finds value in something, don't you?"

Think about that statement for just a moment. Then answer this question: "What were you thinking when you first read the statement?" Were you thinking about something you find value in? Something specific? Pretty crazy, right?

Mind Reading Patterns

This is when we claim to have a certainty and knowing about something we're uncertain of and don't know for sure.

When I tell you: "I know you want to learn conversational hypnosis, because you've purchased this book, and it means you'll do everything necessary and pay any price to master these language patterns completely." Right here I've used several language patterns. I've used cause effect, complex equivalence, universal quanitfiers, and mind reading to name a few of the patterns. The first pattern I used, however, was the mind read pattern: "I know you want to learn conversational hypnosis." How do I know this is true? Maybe you bought this book to giveaway to a friend, and you personally have no interest in learning how to communicate more hypnotically. I am claiming, however, to know something I don't know.

People make these types of statements frequently, and they say them with such conviction and authority or charisma that they are believed to be true by the subject and in some instances people want to believe what the person making the claim is claiming is true.

Double Bind Patterns

The double bind pattern is an illusive choice. It is when I make you think you have a choice by presenting two choices, but really what I want is for you to do something I'm assuming you will do already.

An example of a double bind would be: "After you clean the cat box in a few minutes, are you going to want to ride with me to the store, or stay here instead?" What I'm really wanting is for you to clean the cat box, so what I'm deceptively doing with this language pattern is presupposing you're going to clean it, by asking you after you get finished if you'll want to go to the store with me or stay back instead. Whatever your answer, it doesn't matter, because all I care about is the cat box getting clean, and not cleaning it is not an option—thus you have no choice but to clean it. This is what is meant by illusory choice.

People like to have choices when it comes to deciding to do something or not. This pattern reduces dissonance making it to where the subject is more likely to comply.

Tag Question Patterns

These are questions usually tagged at the end of a sentence to acquire a yes-set agreement frame from the subject. In some cases I have seen conversational hypnotists use tag questions at the beginning and even in the middle of a sentence.

To illustrate what these patterns are consider the following three example:

I.   You want to learn conversational hypnosis, <u>right</u>?

II.   <u>Am I right</u> to assume you want to learn conversational hypnosis?

III.   Conversational hypnosis, <u>am I right</u>, is easy to learn?

As illustrated the tag question is used in all three positions of the sentence. These aren't so bad learning, are they? You can, can you not, learn them without much effort? Isn't it true, you're learning them not? Yes? Terrific! That's what I thought!

Presupposition Patterns

These are linguistic assumptions. When I tell you that learning conversational hypnosis is super easy, because you're actually learning it right now; I have to ask you, "How do I know this?" You'll probably tell me back, "You don't!" At any other time, however, that I might say this to you, you'd likely just agree with me. You'd assume what I was saying by saying "conversational hypnosis is super easy to learn, because you're doing it now," was plausible enough to be true enough to agree with me on.

If I ask you, "When are you going to town?" I'm presupposing you will be going to town at some point in time. I'm assuming! Your answer might be, "I don't know," or "In a few hours," but you're probably more concerned mentally as to why I'm asking this question. You might be assuming I want to ask you a favor or something of the like.

Comparative Deletion Patterns

Now a comparative deletion is when we compare something to nothing. Let me give you an example: "You're getting really good now!" In this statement that I've made I've told you you're getting 'really good'; however, I haven't compared 'really good' to anything you're good at specifically or even generally. I've made an assertion that you're getting really good, but haven't told you what you're really getting good at, have I? This is comparative deletion.

These comparative deletion patterns are interesting because they leave it up to the subject to make their own determination about what it is they're getting good at. Because this statement is so vague and quite general due in part because of the deleted comparison, and in part due to the abstract adjective, you're left mildly confused and as a result disoriented enough to be hypnotized.

Conversational Postulate Patterns

This is when I present you with a "yes/no" question, but it's taken to mean I want you to take some action instead of giving a 'yes' or 'no' reply.

For example: "Can you help me out here and practice these language patterns so that you'll really get this information fully?" The answer to this question is either 'yes' or 'no'; however, you'll likely take this question as an appeal to actually practice these language patterns, am I right?

A tip I'll give you about conversational postulates is something I do quite frequently when I apply them to my subjects. I preface my 'yes/no' sentences with "Would you

___?" I've never had anyone give a 'yes' or 'no' answer, but I did once have a girl tell me, "I guess!" after I'd asked her a conversational postulate type question such as this one.

This is a great compliance pattern.

Lost Performative Patterns

Lost performatives are baseless suppositions. We're inferring importance or something as being necessary only without providing an explanation for why it is important or necessary.

Example: "It's important for you to learn all of these language patterns." What's missing from this statement? The person who or 'performer' making the claim. Note what I'm not saying, "I believe it is important for you to learn all of these language patterns." I'm also not saying in the first example, "John says it's important for you to learn all these language patterns."

No what I've done in the first example is make a claim that you should do something but haven't told you who says it is important for you to learn all these language patterns.

If you later come back and say, "I just made $20,000 this week using only one of the language patterns in this book, so why did you say it was important that I learn them all?" I could come back and say, it wasn't me who made this claim, but some other person. So it protects me from giving bad advice and you later blaming me. When I make such a claim, however, I can make it with absolute conviction and authority to where you 'believe' that is was me making the claim.

Modal Operator Patterns (Necessity/Possibility)

When something is necessary it is a 'must'. When something is a possibility it is a 'should' or 'might'. In other words, when you are told you must do something it makes is absolutely necessary that you do it, for some reason. When you're told you should do something or might want to do something; that is, that it might be a good idea for you to consider, it is perhaps something you may want to put some serious consideration to and possibly act on.

These words like: must, have to, should, can, etc. direct your subject's attention toward something you have in mind for them to consider. In essence, you're controlling their thought.

As a conversational hypnotist there will be times when you want your subject to have certain experiences. These modal operator patterns are one way of directing attention.

For example, in a sales call, it is often times beneficial that you future pace a subject's experience; namely, where you have them picture a future event where they're using the thing you're selling. By asking, "Can you see yourself _____, three months from now, and really, still, enjoying this _____?" If the subject couldn't before, or didn't before, just by now asking this question, using the modal operator of possibility 'can' to preface with, they are in fact 'now' picturing what it is you wanted them to picture in their mind. Be mindful when you use these, as you could find yourself accidentally using them to your detriment in which case you'll not likely get the outcome you're looking for.

Unspecified Verb and Adverb Patterns

This is simply where we have a verb, adverb, or even nominalized verb that is connected to nothing. It leaves us guessing, assuming, or imagining something.

For example, if I say to you, "You're able to do many things," you might ask me back, "What things specifically?" However, the 'you're able to' part of that sentence is me making a statement, but stop for a moment and really consider what I'm saying or rather 'not' saying. I've left out specifically what you're able to do, have I not?

"You're learning these learnings; I know you are!" Now here I've used two language patterns from the Milton Model. I've said, "You're learning these learnings," but what learning, I've unspecified. I've taken a nominalized verb (i.e., to learn) and turned it into 'learnings' and now I'm basically saying that you're learning these learnings. So I've used a nominalization and I've also used an unspecified verb (i.e., learning). What exactly are you learning now? We don't know this, do we?

Incidentally, the other language pattern in that sentence was a 'mind read' pattern. I said, "I know you are." The question begets how do I know you are?

Lack of Referential Index Patterns

This is when a phase has a deleted subject that cannot be referenced back to any noun or classified grouping, per se. I could say, for example, "One has all the knowledge within them already to master hypnotic storytelling. I know this to be true."

Now here I've used several language patterns, but the one important to teach you about lack of referential index was the first word I used in the sentence, i.e. 'one'.

The word 'one' is very general and lacks reference. The question becomes, "Which 'one'?" Yet, the subject hears me say 'one' and understands that to mean 'everyone'. There really is no reference as to who the 'one' references, is there? I could actually have just as easily said 'two' or 'three' or 'four' people, could not I?

Pacing and Leading Patterns

Pacing and leading are used by conversational hypnotists and hypnotic storytellers all the time, frequently in fact, in conversations regularly. Pacing is when you express a truism in successive order to obtain a 'yes-set' from the subject.

When someone is in the constant habit of repetitively and consecutively agreeing with us it is difficult for them to disagree with us when we state something only plausible, or even untrue. It's our human conditioning and the 'other mind' making sense of unconscious patterns.

Leading is when we express a plausible suggestion or idea on the backend of a couple or few pacing statements.

So far you've gotten this far with language patterns in this book. You've also learned things you haven't learnt in other books. It is easy to use pacing and leading statements. You'll, I know, find this to be true, will you not?

In the preceding paragraph I've used pacing and leading statements to communicate with you and some are true and valid, while some are only plausible; yet, it's easy to agree when I use a tag question onto a leading statement, right?

Extended Quote Patterns (Stacking Realities)

Extended quotes are when you nest quotes said by other people inside of quotes inside of quoted, etc. In many instances utilizing this particular language pattern will create confusion and allow you to more easily bypass a subject's critical faculty, i.e. their resistance mechanism.

I was talking to my father the other day. He told me he had talked to my Uncle John. Uncle John said Aunt Madeline didn't really know what she was doing, so she consulted a repair man for a particular machine in her home. I was told by someone. It may have been my father. No, maybe not him. Maybe Aunt Madeline. Anyway, it was a washing machine my father told me. That's right it was him and not her. But now everything is fine since my Uncle John knew him, and ensured that everything was done right after he met up with me that Friday. The repair man was a nice guy.

Do you see in the above paragraph how I stacked different realities and nested several extended quotes to create confusion?

Remember that confusion is like shock or surprise in that it can help us to bypass people's critical thinking mind to get ideas and suggestions into the 'other mind'.

Ambiguity Patterns (Phonologic, Punctuation, Syntactic, Scope)

Phonological ambiguity are simply words that sound the same, but which have different means. For example, when speaking, I could say, "You're unconscious," or I could say, "Your unconscious," and it would be difficult to determine with clarity what was meant. This is especially useful for the conversational hypnotist when speaking in heavy abstracts. These words that sound alike are known linguistically as homophones. The words that have the same sound and spelling are referred to linguistically as homonyms—for example, "To stalk a person using the stalk of a deadly plant, is perhaps, the worst type of stalking a stalker might engage in to engage the sought out victim."

Punctuational ambiguity is when I say, "I'm telling you something now nothing really happens does it?" What I've just done is create a run-on sentence without putting down any punctuation. When you read this sentence it may have been slightly confusing, and this is why. The sentence should have read: "I'm telling you something now. Nothing really happens does it.?" In a conversational context, and not a written context, this type of punctuational ambiguity can be done by emphasizing certain parts of the sentence. Periods and commas are used to represent where natural pauses occur in a sentence and to break a sentence down to make it grammatically correct.

For you could say: "I'm telling you something. Now nothing really happens, does it?" Notice for effect I've broken the sentence with a period before the 'now' instead of after.

Syntactic ambiguity is when you take a sentence and you construct it to mean something other than what it was intended to mean. One sentence may therefore be determined to have multiple meanings; explicitly, to communicate different ideas in a way that confuses the message receiver, because now they are now confused by what the meaning should be.

For example: "Hypnotizing hypnotists can be hypnotizing." This is an example of a syntactic ambiguity. Syntax is word order. In this case the order confuses the meaning because multiple meanings can be construed. In this case is the person making the statement insinuating they get confused when they hypnotize other hypnotists or is the meaning to say that hypnotists who hypnotize are hypnotizing? It's ambiguous to say the least.

Scope ambiguity is the last form of ambiguity mentioned in the Milton Model. Scope ambiguity is something as simple as saying like: "I want you to think about a pen standing up." The scope is unclear. First of all there are two types of ambiguity going on in this particular construction. One of phonological because you don't know exactly what I mean by a 'pen'? It could be a writing instrument, it could be a bobby pen, if could be a tack board pin, it could be stick pin, that is, and so on. You might, even assume I am talking a person named pen. Anything is possible, but the scope dimension is also present in this construction. The scope happens when I ask you to "...think about a pen standing up." Am I asking you to stand up while you think about a pen, or am I asking you to think about an actual pen that is fictitiously growing legs and arms and picking itself up and standing up? So the scope is clearly unclear; thus, ambiguous.

Metaphor and Simile Patterns

Milton Erickson used metaphors and similes as he talked with his psychotherapy clients. He used these brilliantly to convey ambiguous ideas to his subject's other mind to force their critical mind out of the way and have them enter a thoughtful state of reflective contemplation.

When you say something is something else; that is, comparing two things as actually the same category or class of thing each is, then this is a metaphor. For example if I tell you: "My dog is a beast!" What do you draw from this statement? Do you think my dog acts like a beast? Do you think my dog looks like a beast? Do you think my dog and a beast are one and the same? I'm expressing that the creature that is my dog is also a creature that represents what a beast is. This is metaphor where you compare something to something else metaphorically connecting the one to the latter.

When you say something like: "My dog is like a beast." In this case we're not actually saying that the dog is a beast; rather, we're portraying the dog to have certain aspects which are similar in nature to the concept of what a beast represents.

Interestingly enough unless we define the qualities and attributes of what we mean by when we say 'beast' this makes for a rather ambiguous metaphor or simile that could be construed as quite confusing causing trance to happen in our subject.

Stories are powerful vehicles for invoking emotional responses in our subjects, and getting them to empathize with the heroine or protagonist in ways that they feel less threatened by. A story is just a story by the way and therefore people can get emotionally transported without fear that they will lose their dignity or self-worth. Stories allow us to communicate many things on many levels of consciousness.

THE META MODEL

We've touched a tiny bit on the Meta Model and what it is. Now we'll go into a bit more detail. The way I like to metaphorically perceive the Meta Model as being is like a train tunnel with two sets of rail tracks going through the tunnel. One set of tracks are for trains departing you, and one set of tracks are for trains traveling toward you.

The more away from you something becomes, the more abstract it is perceived. The closer the train nears toward you, the less ambiguous, and more specific and into focus, the train becomes.

The Meta Model is the train approaching you. The Milton Model is the train leaving you behind. The more aware you are of a train the less hypnotized you are. The more unaware of a train you are, because it's so far away, and hence defocused the more hypnotized you become when involving yourself in thoughts of it.

It is easy to focus on the Meta Model Train, because it is always right there in front of you where you can see it, focus on it, know it specifically, and so on. It is difficult and you're defocused when you're trying your hardest to think about and imagine the Milton Model because it is far out of site. A distant memory. No longer in your reality.

If I were to ask you to consider hypothetically what color the third car on the Milton Model Train is you might think its blue, or possibly yellow, or claim you have no idea what I'm talking about. That train has you defocused, meaning that you're unable to make perfect sense of it. The harder you try to make sense of something so outside your periphery the more defocused you become and the more difficult it is for you to give an answer.

On the other hand if I were to ask you to consider hypothetically what color is the third car of the Meta Model Train you have no problem telling me that it's a rusty brown color, because the car is front and center right in front of you. You can see it. It is in perfect focus. It's right there in your reality. You're able to see it perfectly. You can describe it for me in specific detail.

These two models the Milton Model and the Meta Model are representative of these two trains and the experiences you have when you're able to focus on something or find something quite defocused and so artfully vague that you cannot help but enter the hypnotic state.

This is a rather interesting phenomenon that happens when something is defocused and blurry and we try our hardest to focus on it to make sense of it. Our attention in these instances is fully captured. Capturing attention, we have mentioned in brief, in this book, is one of the steps involved in the process of conversational hypnosis. When we're able to look at something that is crystal clear our tendency is to dismiss it without paying much attention to it. This is what I mean by the NLP train coming toward you. You can see it so clearly that you take it for granted and assume it will always be there for you to observe, so why bother focusing on it.

So something defocused is hypnotic because we want to focus on it but can't. Something focused is less hypnotic because we see it all the time and have no reason to wish for it in our lives or to even think about it. Keep all this in mind.

Now I want to talk a little more about the Meta Model. It was first published in 1975. I've told you by Dr. John Grinder and Dr. Richard Bandler. In 1997 Bandler commissioned L. Michael Hall, another NLPer in the industry, to add nine more meta model forms to the Meta Model, which is the Meta Model Extended we use today in the world of NLP.

The Meta Model was modeled after three highly successful psychiatrists; namely, Fritz Pearl, Milton H. Erickson, and family therapist Virginia Satir. So this model for this reason is not exactly the inverse of the Milton Model; however, since Erickson was one of the people being modeled, this sheds light, and expectation, on why many of the patterns are the same as in the Milton Model.

Simple Deletion Violation Patterns

The first simple deletion occurs when people cite unspecified nouns. An example might be: "You suck!" The person who is called 'you' is unknown or unspecified. To challenge such a violation you might ask: "Specifically who are you referring to when you say 'you'?" or you might ask: "Suck what specifically?"

The next form of simple deletion are vague nouns or pronouns that are ambiguous and which cause confusion for the listener. An example might be: "You need to wake up and smell the roses." To challenge this type of violation you might ask back: "Which roses, specifically?

The next from of simple deletion are unspecified adjectives. An example might be: "That's a stupid car." To challenge this type of violation you might ask back: "How do you know the car is stupid?" or "How do you educate a car to make it smart?" When the subject says, "I don't know." They might themselves feel stupid, and they might question their judgment of the car."

The next type of simple deletion are unspecified relationships. These are assumed relationships that two or more ideas are assumed to have. An example would be: "I can't help you until I walk my dog." To challenge this type of violation you might ask back: "Have you ever helped someone without walking your dog?"

The next form of simple deletion are comparative deletions. These occur when the message sender leaves out the object that should be associated with the comparison. An example is: "You're better than that." The challenge to such a violation might be to ask: "Better than what specifically?" or "Better how, compared to what exactly?"

Unspecified Referential Index Violation Patterns

These are phrases which delete the 'actor' being referenced. These often occur when a group is generally referenced. An example might be: "People should be able to do
more than just go to work every day." To question such a
violation one might ask back: "Which people are you referring to?"

Another example might be the generalization: "Americans are money hungry!" To which you might ask:
"Which Americans are specifically hungry for money?"

Unspecified Verb Violation Patterns

Unspecified verbs patterns are process words which are
missing their descriptors; that is, verbs which are unspecified. These patterns are ones that can include the omis-
sion of verbs and or their objects.

An example might be when someone says something
like: "Don't make me leave." In this example the object is
missing and the verb is unspecified; that is, the location
the person happens to be, and the location they would
leave for, but also the reason as to why they might be leaving in the first place, yet also the verb 'make' is unspecified,
requiring the object which would provide the 'how' or 'in
what way' the person would be making this person leave.
This type of violation may be challenged by asking a simple clarification type questions, such as: "Make me leave
how?" or "Leave to go where, exactly?"

Nominalization Violation Patterns

Now we transition into the second part of this model, where we transition away from 'deletion' and toward 'generalizations'. A nominalization, as I mentioned while expounding on the Milton Model is a verb, adverb, or even adjective which has been converted from a process into a solid concrete object or noun. This is commonly done by simply adding endings like, '–ing' to the end of a verb, and possibly an 's' on to the '–ing' ending, i.e. '–ings'.

An example of a process (action verb) being nominalized might be: "Do you understand these understandings?" where 'understand' is the action verb, and 'understandings' is the nominalized noun.

People usually hold a high regard for objects they can feel attached to. Something fleeting; namely, a verb, is something that can escape us and create the sensation of a loss happening, etc., which could cause a depression to set in or some similar emotion.

To challenge a nominalized generalization violation you might ask of this example: "What is specifically meant to be understood?" converting the nominalization back into a process. You might also follow up by asking: "What do you understand?" where the answer given would be clarity about what they expect you to understand. You see the noun 'understandings' is too generalized and doesn't give a rational explanation about what specifically should be understood, expectation-wise. You ask questions to challenge this violation so you gain clarity and force someone to be more explicit.

Modal Operator Violation Patterns

In the Milton Model we covered two such types of modal operator patterns, and now we'll look at more. Modal operators are words which dictate or imply what is possible, right, or even essential. The forms we'll look at now are: 'necessity', 'plausibility', 'judgment', and 'contingency'.

Necessity is when someone generalizes without clarification that something is pertinent or necessary to happen—for example, the violation: "You have to tell me the truth now!" The words 'have to' are the modal operator in this sentence. They can be challenged by asking: "What will happen if I don't?" The answer then given will determine why this action is a necessity, or bring light to the message deliverer why it might not be necessary at all.

Possibility is when someone generalizes without clarification that something is possible to do, implying that it should be done. These types of modal operators are usually used to softly or more permissively tell someone to do something to do. The point of using them is to take away the likelihood they will not reject being told what to do, as often people don't like to be told what to do and will rebel against an order.

An example might be: "You can keep studying these linguistic language patterns after you've finished the book through." In this example there is a presupposition secretly hid, which hint at and implies that the reader (e.g., you) will in fact finish reading this book. However, the modal operator is actually the word 'can' which is used to imply that you the reader should keep studying these language patterns, without me telling you to study them. A challenge to this type of violation would be to ask me: "What would happen if I didn't keep studying them?"

Judgment is when someone generalizes without clarification that something uses a 'lost performative' to create a judgment that you should do something because it's the 'right' thing to do. These are used often in conversation and actually in minute ways bring to the surface the moral ethical code of the person making such a judgment. It also highlights their values and gives a glimpse into their map of the world. It should be noted that these judgments are not always necessarily 'right' or 'wrong' but merely beliefs held by an individual.

An example of a judgment modal operator pattern might be: "You should have a better understanding by now." In this example the 'lost performative' is that which the subject should have an understanding of by now. In this example I have also presented a nominalization pattern, which is 'understanding', which should be familiar to you from an earlier example I presented you with. The modal operator in the example here is the word 'should' implying judgment on the idea someone 'should' have accomplished having done something. I covertly made a judgment myself, when I put to you, the reader: "…which should be familiar to you from an earlier example…" again using the modal operator of judgment 'should' to imply judgment on what you should have already learnt.

Other judgment modal operators are words like: 'ought to, 'ought not to' and 'should not'.

Contingency is when someone makes a statement to suggest generally something else that might be an alternative. These are usually used as a contingency plan of attack on someone or to have someone consider the alternative of why they might want to comply having them think about what is inferred to likely happen if they don't comply.

An example might be: "I wouldn't do that if I were you." The modal operator of contingency is the word 'wouldn't' which is used here to infer some negative consequence might happen if they do what it is they're thinking they will do. Notice the intention behind why a communicator might use this type of contingency modal operator is to have them think twice about doing something they're planning on doing. These can be very persuasive in having the subject comply with your suggestions. People want to avoid negative consequences psychologically to minimize the dissonance that is likely to result.

To challenge these violations you might ask: "Why would you not do it if you were me?" or "What exactly will happen if I do?" or "Why would you be me?" These types of challenges spin the frame around and reframes the situation to gain clarity from such a broad generalization. It also chunks down specifically to have the person making such a declarative statement justify specifically what will happen if you don't do something. In many instances the certainty something will happen is uncertain and only plausible, not certain.

Many times when I've challenged these violations the person I'm challenging will end up agreeing that my action is likely the best choice compared to their logical fallacy.

Universal Quantifier Violation Patterns

These are words that have no referential index which are absolute generalizations. For example someone might say: "My dad never trusts my decisions." In this example a specific example is not referenced, and the person making the declaration is citing an absolute generalization.

These types of words are: 'always,' 'never,' 'every,' 'all,' 'none,' 'only,' 'everyone,' 'no one,' and 'nobody'.

When these words are used in a sentence the inference is that in no case ever is something possible or able to occur. In the example above the argument is that the person's father 'never' trusts his or her decisions. It is impossible to say that the father will never ever trust his or her decision in the future, because the future hasn't happened. Also it is natural to think that there have been instances that this person's father has trusted them at some point in the past.

To challenge such a generalization usually all that is required is to emphasize the universal quantifier, i.e. 'never'. In the example about the dad never trusting, you might come back and challenge with: "Your dad NEVER trusts your decisions?" Often times when you challenge something like this it will cause the communicator to do a trans-derivational search (TDS) in which they scan their memory to look for instances of when their father did in fact trust them to make a decision. This can actually lessen the argument they've made and actually bring better thoughts to spring up about their father.

Presupposition Violation Patterns

Now we start to transition away from generalization and move into distortions. In communication people distort meaning and inherently infer things for the purpose of making half-truths make sense. In doing so meanings are distorted as well as communication.

Presuppositions are a statement made that does not contain all its parts though they're inherently inferred for the argument to make sense.

An example of a presupposition might be: "You're not going to find it anywhere, so why waste your time looking?" In this example something is inferred as being lost and never to be found again. The person presenting this argument is also saying that because of this fact (it is not a fact by the way) the person should give up looking for the object missing. Inferring the person will 'never' find it takes us back to the universal quantifier violation. How does the person know it will never be found? Are they inferring they've done something with the lost object in order to know this as a fact? They are also saying that it is a waste of time to look for something they believe will never be found again. In this violation the person making the argument is presupposing looking for something lost is a waste of time.

To challenge this violation one might ask: How do you know where the object is? (Inferring that knowing it will not be found must mean they know where it is.) You might also say: "What will I find if I don't waste my time?" making the argument flip on its head that wasted time is when you look for something you won't find; therefore not looking means finding something you're missing.

Selectional Restriction Violation Patterns

This violation happens when the communicator attributes a conscious attribute to a lifeless object. An example might be: "You're car is happy now that you've finally put fresh oil in it." To challenge this violation simply ask: "How can a car be happy?"

Milton Erickson once used a selectional restriction violation pattern on a terminally ill patient, saying: "A tomato plant can feel good, Joe."

Cause Effect Violation Pattern

Earlier we said cause effect patterns are when someone says something like: "I went to the store, because I needed bread." It can just as easily be worded semantically: "I needed bread, so I went to the store." Both are cause and effect statements that mean the same thing. The only difference is the bridge-word has changed from 'because' to 'so'. This may seem like a valid and justifiable argument; however, there very well could be other solutions which would have been possible to cause the person making the statement not to have to go to the store. Perhaps someone else could have gone instead? This is known as reframing the argument to shed more light on other alternatives which might be a better solution eliminating the causal quality of the statement.

Another type of cause effect violation happens when someone assumes that one thing causes another or is caused by another without any logical or provable sensory based evidence to support the causal connection—for example: "When you don't let me talk, I feel unimportant." This violation can be challenged by asking a question like: "How does your choice to believe I won't let you talk make you feel unimportant; that is to say, are you saying I have the power to control how you feel?"

In this type of example the person making the argument might have to rethink their logic to determine their statement is illogical; explicitly, realizing there is no evidence to support a causal connection.

Mind Reading Violation Patterns

This type of violation distortion is caused when someone asserts that they believe to know the feelings, meanings, intentions, motivations, actions, beliefs, or thoughts of another without any logical or rational explanation that proves they know this.

Believe it or not these types of patterns are used all the time by people. They are used habitually, in fact. For example someone says, "My father is getting older and harder and harder to take care of," and someone else listening says, "I know exactly how you feel. My dog has diabetes and I now have to give him insulin shots." The statement: "I know exactly how you feel," cannot be proven, and therefore this person making this assertion is engaging in using a mind read violation pattern.

To challenge this type of violation it is possible by asking a question like: "How do you know how I feel?" or you could ask, "Are you a mind reader? How is your experience my experience?"

There are other mind reading violations such as when someone claims to know what an outcome will be (e.g., "I know he'll fail that test." / "How specifically do you know he'll fail that test?") or claiming to believe that you or someone else will have a certain futuristic outcome that could be an absolute future outcome (e.g., "I'll never get the job of my dreams?" / "Are you absolutely certain you never will?"). As I've done in the last example given I've actually stacked another Meta Model violations with the Mind Reading violation. Keep in mind often people will use more than one violation when communicating. When people combine these types of violations with mind reading violation patterns they are fundamentally psychologizing; that is, where they take on the role of a psychotherapist and make futuristic predictions about someone else's life without having the qualifications of a licensed and trained professional. Some psychics often assume this role in their profession.

Complex Equivalence Violation Patterns

These are statements, ideas, or experiences that do not relate equally, which are grouped together as interrelated and therefore construed as synonymous to one another. An example might be: "The cat went outside when I opened the door to get something, meaning he's upset with me." Here the cat going outdoors is stated as being equal to him being upset with his/her owner. This can also be viewed as a mind reading pattern in which the owner is claiming to know what the cat is feeling. The complex equivalence violation occurs when the word 'meaning' is used to state that the cat going outside is equivalent to him/her being upset with the owner. This isn't necessarily a true statement since the cat may be going outside for a different reason, i.e. to catch a mouse?

To challenge this violation you might ask: "Every instance in which your cat goes outside means he's upset with you?" or you might ask: "Is every outside cat upset with pet owners in general or only your cat?" or "Do all cats go outside when they're upset?"

Lost Performative Violation Patterns

Lost performative violations occur when someone communicates a value judgment without clearly referencing whom has made the judgment. In other words, the 'performer' or 'actor' is missing from the argument.

An example of a lost performative might be: "This is the way you roof a house!" This judgment is distorted because there's nobody to reference as having made this claim, nor is an opinion a fact. To challenge a lost performative violation you might ask: "According to whom?" When you do the person must either take credit for the argument which can then be disputed, or attribute the claim to somebody else. By attributing to someone else this would cause some dissociation from the 'actor' perhaps creating greater credibility or more interest in how they might have come to that conclusion about how to roof a house. One thing is for certain is that you'd not likely be able to argue the point, except with the person who happened to share it with you. On the other hand, should the person take credit for making the claim, you could challenge them by asking: "How did you arrive at that understanding?"

Either/Or Violation Patterns

As I mentioned to you earlier in this chapter Dr. Richard Bandler commissioned L. Michael Hall to extend the original Meta Model with more recently discovered pattern violations. The rest of these patterns will be his contribution to the Meta Model.

An either/or violation is a question or direct statement that focuses attention on a consequence that assumes (i.e., presupposes) something else, giving an illusive choice.

For example: "Are you going to go get me some food, or just stay bored bothering me all day for no apparent reason?" It appears that a choice is being given, however, what's going on is an inference that the person receiving the message will be bothering the person if they don't go and get them some food. There's an illusive choice presented presumptively; namely: either get food, or you're bothering me. So in this case the person is claiming someone is bothering them, but inferring that if they go get them food they'll not be a bother anymore. Asking this in a question format requires an answer of one or the other; however, other choices could be possible, but it is inferred that these are the only choices available to consider. To challenge this violation the receiver might ask: "Are those my only options?" or "Am I not able to ___?"

Over/Under Violation Patterns

Over/under violations are nomenclatures that depend on abstract definitions that don't reference anything or anyone in particular. These terminologies depend on multiple intensities of indirection and incline to produce abstractions in the mind that sends a person into the hypnotic state. The tendency for people interpreting these terms is to think of them as real and not as what they are which are concepts.

An example would be: "I bought an elephant so I could get to sleep at night." The challenge to this violation could be: "How does an elephant cause you to sleep?"

Delusional Verbal Split Violation Patterns (Elementalism)

These violations occur when people compartmentalize parts of a whole. Some common examples are use people/personality, time, space, emotions, energy, matter, and mind.

An example might be: "Part of me hates change, yet another part of me embraces it." To challenge this violation you might ask: "How would you feel if both parts of you were aligned and whole?"

Multiordinality Violation Patterns (Nominalization)

These violations occur when someone takes an extremely broad interpretation of the meaning of words to the point where a word can take on countless meanings and be used 'ad infinitum'.

For example: "I just want to be hateful for the sake of being hateful." In this example the person is using the word hateful as cause for acting hateful. Another example is often when someone says something similar to: "I love you because I love you."

To challenge this type of violation you can ask questions like: "How hateful do you want to be?" which will denote the varying qualities of hatefulness forcing them to see the limitation and stopping the effects of reuse. With the example of love you can ask: "Are you unable to love me for any other reason?" You now see that this is putting a limitation challenging them to see other alternatives; thus, limiting the argument.

Static Word Violation Patterns (Nominalization)

These are terms with fixed or rigid meanings. These terms express ideas or views as if they are absolute truths everyone should know and be expected to follow. These terms usually are not rooted in logic and have no basis of fact to them.

For example: "Get used to it, because that's the way it is around here," said by someone asserting authoritatively something as though it is an absolute undeniable truth. In this example, and we see these used often for the purpose of controlling people, people tend to want to dominate an idea in someone else's head to limit them and make them feel trapped by a condition.

To challenge such a violation you might ask: "How do you mean by it?" or "How do you know it will not be another way?" By challenging in this way it causes a trans-derivational search in the mind of the controller which paints a possibility; breaking down the 'absoluteness' of the argument.

Pseudo-Word Violation Patterns (Nominalization)

These are linguistic maps that reference nothing conceptual or in which exists in an external reality.

For example: "I can't get outstanding now." In this example the person is asserting that there's something that can be achieved which is called 'outstanding' and they're unable to get it (whatever 'outstanding' is).

To challenge such a violation you may ask them to elaborate on what that means by asking something like: "If I could get 'outstanding' what would that look like for me?" By taking this approach you're causing them to define specifically what is meant by such an abstraction.

Identification Violation Patterns (Nominalization)

The term 'identity' roots down to mean 'the same' and no separate things are ever completely the same; meaning, 'identification' is actually an abstract concept that results from deleting distinctions of comparison.

For example someone might cry out in a bout of emotional uprising: "I hate my life." In this example the person making the statement is claiming to identify with something called 'life' which is a nominalization, but one they've taken a particular identification to understand.

To challenge this violation you might ask them: "How are you different aside from the 'you' you hate?" This challenge takes them outside thinking that they are this thing called 'life'.

Emotionalizing Violation Patterns

These violations happen when someone uses their emotions to collect and deal out information to others abstractly, but inferring indirectly how they are feeling, by actually dissociating away from the cause of their feelings.

For example someone says, "Today's been upsetting." They are insinuating that they are upset and it occurred at some point in their day by some externality that happened as a result of some event of occurrence.

To challenge this type of violation you might ask: "How do you mean? Are you 'yourself' upset because today is 'today' and if so will you be upset tomorrow?" In challenging in this way you'll get to the root of the problem more likely.

Personalizing Violation Patterns

This is when someone takes what another says as a personal attack on them—taking it personally. An example might be: "That restaurant doesn't serve grill-cheeses anymore, because they want to piss me off!"

To challenge this type of assertion you might ask: "If they decide to start serving it again is it because they love you?" or "Might they have stopped carrying grill-cheeses for any other reason?"

Metaphor Violation Patterns

Sometimes people will use metaphors to suggest someone is experiencing life in a certain light. They might use a metaphor to indirectly elicit a trans-derivational search for the purpose of focusing someone's attention in a particular direction—often time a limited position.

For example: "You are a lonely boat lost at sea during a raging storm." This type of metaphor may be used to insinuate the person is weak, lonely, and lost, when actually they're not. However, by casting out a metaphor in this way the person may begin believing this about themselves.

To challenge such a violation and release the control of the metaphor over you, you might ask: "What type of boat, specifically?" In asking this it takes the focus off the emotional aspects of the metaphor and shifts it to more logical and rational; that is, 'critical' type thinking. Using critical thinking faculties the person may decide consciously they are not the metaphor or what it represents.

INDIRECT HYPNOSIS LANGUAGE PATTERNS

The following indirect hypnosis language patterns are presented here to you for the purpose of helping you start to speak more hypnotically.

One doesn't have to memorize them all at once, you can take your time and learn them one at a time until you master them all. As astonishing as these patterns are they will prove themselves more when you use them to conversationally hypnotize other people; meaning, you'll get a first-hand glimpse of the power you'll hold over other people just by using your language more effectively.

And in what way will you memorize these? I wonder this as I think about you studying these patterns. You should remember that these language patterns are very hypnotic in nature and using them you might drop into a trance as well. It's as if you just can't help but zone out while you study these patterns.

Again, you don't have to memorize all seven of these patterns right now. I tell reiterate this because it's as if some people find they are familiar to them before they ever consider memorizing them, and thus memorize them now. You should remember you use these all the time unconsciously, so if you find it necessary to memorize them all now, that's as perfect as it gets.

Seven Hypnotic Language Patterns

I.   One doesn't have to (name) ____.

Example: One doesn't have to (John) go into a trance.

Purport: This is a great language pattern for introducing an embedded command to the 'other mind'. When you add in a person's name it personalizes the command to them.

II.   It's as if ___.

Example: It's as if you just drop into a trance.

Purport: This is a great language pattern for introducing an embedded command to the 'other mind'. It's as if you can easily remember it also.

III.   You should remember ___.

Example: You should remember how easy it is to drop into a trance.

Purport: This is a great language pattern for introducing an embedded command to the 'other mind'. The word remember, like most –re words, are trance inducing because they have a person shift back in time to another experience.

IV.   I wonder ___.

Example: I wonder deep into a trance you'll go?

Purport: When you wonder your subject wonders also; that is to say, they wonder about what you're wondering about. This is a great pattern for directing attention.

V.   And in what way will you ___?

Example: And in what way will you remember these patterns, I wonder.

Purport: When you ask someone 'how' or 'in what way' they will they do something it forces them mentally to think about it, i.e. a trans-derivational search, and in the process of visualizing it, they see how they will.

VI.   Meaning ___.

Example: You're studying these patterns; meaning, you're memorizing them now.

Purport: The word 'meaning' is a complex equivalent which is essentially saying that something is 'equal' to something else. If it slightly plausible, or your subject is in well hypnotized, and it's not at all plausible, the subject will associate whatever two ideas together and assimilate them unconsciously.

VII.   ___as [adjective/adverb] as ___

Example: You're memorizing these patterns as instantly as you are.

Purport: This pattern links two clauses together. The pattern is similar and does what a typical conjunction would do to link to clauses, yet, does is more hypnotically.

Seven is a great start for remembering all of these patterns. I wonder, in what way, will you remember only these seven patterns? Meaning, you should remember them all as quickly as possible. It's as if they're easy to remember, don't you think? One doesn't have to put forth much effort, does one? You should remember to use them often; meaning, you'll learn them as soon as possible, this way. In what way you will learn all seven doesn't have to make you want to as instantly as you learn other things learn these; meaning, these seven patterns are very easy to retain and master now.

If you haven't noticed, by now, these seven language patterns were covertly used in the first part of this section on indirect hypnosis language patterns. These may have evaded your radar, meaning you weren't conscious they were being used on you indirectly to help you learn them more quickly—they were used on you though.

Many more of these types of hypnotic language patterns have been used on you throughout this book. My recommendation to the serious hypnotic storyteller or conversational hypnotist is that you immediately visit www.indirectknowledge.com and purchase one or all of the many hypnotic language flashcard decks that are offered up for sale. These flashcard decks will help you learn and master speaking hypnotically by repetitively having you study hypnotically the indirect hypnosis language patterns you'll find on the various decks. Soon there will be a deck customized specifically for this book you're reading now. As soon as they become available I would if I were you rush out and buy a deck for yourself. It will definitely give you an advantage over everybody else and make your much more hypnotic in how you communicate and tell hypnotic stories.

The Recap

Hypnotic language is twofold; namely, direct and indirect. The Milton Model is the indirect model that can be used to imply meaning, without directly coming out and explicitly stating directly what is meant. In this way, using this model allows you to communicate on multiple levels of consciousness with your hypnotic subjects, and allows your subject to create the 'right' meanings inside their mind that will be most advantageous to the hypnotic storyteller. It's the same thing that happens when we read a book with no pictures and automatically envision the characters and what they might look like in our mind. We naturally fill in the gaps where information being communicated is distorted, deleted, or generalized.

The second model is the Meta Model. Some people perceive this as the inverse to the Meta Model, but it is much more than this. Keep in mind it was formed also by some of the indirect language patterns used by Milton Erickson, but also keep in mind that it was modeled after some of the other expertly successful therapists working during the same time. This model is useful for having us communicate more explicitly while telling our hypnotic stories, but also allows us to call out other people when they violate certain linguistic loopholes. So when someone generalizes and makes the assumption that 'everybody' does something that they are suggesting, it allow us to raise the red flag and question critically the statement made by them. In this way we become consciously critical when other people are using hypnotic storytelling or conversational hypnosis on us to achieve their own outcomes.

Lastly we covered some powerful hypnotic language patterns that I've provided you with for the sake of getting you started practicing speaking more hypnotically. These of course are only seven of many cookie-cutter fill-in-the-blank patterns that you may wish to purchase on our website: www.indirectknowledge.com. They definitely make learning and speaking hypnotically much easier and automatic. They work because they require repetition which itself is hypnosis inducing. You'll discover as you're flipping through the flashcards that you're learning using your 'hypnotic mind' while also utilizing your 'critical thinking'. This combined approach drastically lessens the learning curve and makes it so you accelerate your learning in a micro-fraction of the time it would otherwise take you to learn these hypnotic mind changing persuasion patterns. Trust me on this!

The Next Step

Academically, I can tell you the step-by-step logic of the psychological principles applied to hypnotic storytelling;

namely, as it relates to Hypnotic Language. However, I know it wouldn't make you a better hypnotic storyteller, just more knowledgeable on this subject matter.

As I've mentioned I believe that learning comes by doing, and testing for yourself the lessons in this book. I think all learning first happens at the unconscious level, and that the conscious mind takes more time to catch up to what you already have learnt unconsciously, already.

With hypnotic storytelling you have already inside you the knowledge and learnings to be able to capably well tell hypnotic stories. In truth, you already tell hypnotic stories without even being aware when you do.

This book walks you through the process of hypnotic storytelling in a unique way that brings with it clarity. It is better not to overthink Hypnotic Storytelling, the Zeirgarnik Effect, Nested Loop Sequences, and Hypnotic Language, because as soon as you do, you stop being quite so hypnotic.

These exercises will help prepare you to tell hypnotic stories without your critical thinking getting in the way. The 'hypnotic mind' is the 'other mind' which has already learnt the Hypnotic Hero's Journey Model, the Hypnotic Language Predicates that linguistically and affectively construct hypnotic realities from the hypnotic stories you tell using them, that I've presented to you, even the Zeirgarnik Effect, Hypnotic Nested Loop Sequences, and Hypnotic Fractionation that can be implemented into your hypnotic stories, and now Hypnotic Language. I ask you to suspend your disbelief and trust in the process, and let your stories hypnotize your subjects naturally. Play with using the hypnotic language patterns I've given you to study, as well as the Milton Model and Meta Model to be able to discover in your own mind experientially where your mind travels, and how your subject's react as you layer hypnotic language into your hypnotic stories. Consider this blind faith in your 'hypnotic mind' comparable to riding a bicycle you've already learnt to ride. You might at any moment mount a bicycle in the future and ride it without your conscious mind's interference—astonishingly! In the same way, think about now using these hypnotic language patterns to do the same and position yourself as an amazingly hypnotic, hypnotic storyteller.

Have a think about that as you become dumbfounded by your 'hypnotic mind's' ability to affect real change in others—gaining you what you want.

I.   Memorize the seven hypnotic language patterns and layer them into the five hypnotic stories you drafted back in chapter 4's 'next step' section. Then practice telling your nested loop stories with these language patterns and watch for yourself how much more hypnotic your stories now are.

II.   Hypnotize everyone you come into contact with conversationally using the artfully vague Milton Model patterns. If you have purchased any of the hypnotic language flashcard decks from indirectknowledge.com practice using them as well, as it will be easier for you to hypnotize people using the cookie-cutter fill-in-the-blank patterns.

III.   Be mindful of other people's language patterns and using the Meta Model violations call people out on their linguistic constructions whenever they distort, delete, or generalize information ambiguously subtracting from the direct meaning they are trying to communicate. Doing this will really help you achieve a mastery of critically analyzing other people's inherent language patterns.

CHAPTER 6

NLP AND HYPNOTIC STORYTELLING

The hypnotic mind is the mind that you're not going to really be able to understand its structure and function, or even be able to perceive how it operates lucidly, for that matter. There are many models of the subconscious mind, unconscious mind, other mind, or whatever you want to call it; however, these models are merely 'attempts' to defining it, what is an abstractions, in a way that can be logically rationalized for the purpose of bringing some clarity to some of the aspects of what I label the: 'hypnotic mind'. I urge you to keep in mind that the 'hypnotic mind' is not rational, nor does it operate in a way that is easily understood. You see it's conceptual, and emotional, and hypnotic, and so much more than this, and probably more than we will ever cognitively understand it to be.

When you're in the hypnotic state you're tapped into its power, wonderment, hypnotisms, supernatural qualities, and otherworldly characteristics that are more psychic and felt than they are logically perceived. I hope you, the reader, get my meaning on some level.

Anyhow, this 'hypnotic mind' may not make much sense perceptually, but conceptually it is dreamlike and hypnotic and what is the astonishment of a child's playful pretend and make believe world is all about, and, yes, that's right, even more than this and not.

I want you to think about how easy it is for a child to tap into this 'hypnotic mind'; that is, their imagination. Inside this imagination are plastic realities, worlds of make believe and pretend, that the child play-acts and creates without critical thinking getting in the way and hindering what's possible for them.

Let's talk now about children are able to tap into their 'hypnotic mind' so effortlessly, while many adults find it rather difficult to do so. Play attention, this is important!...

Okay, so we learnt some about this thing, this filter, this thing I call the 'critical faculty' which is a metaphoric mechanism that 'critically thinks' about everything coming in through the five senses.

Remember that old cliché: "What you see is what you get!" Yes, this would be something the 'critical faculty' would love to believe is true. But, if you started talking about how unicorns exist and gods and goddesses then your critical faculty might not like you very much; in fact, it might reject those ideas rather instantly. I mean, after all, it's not practical to believe in such things, is it? Or is it? I don't know, I'm asking you!

Reader, if you're going into a hypnotic trance right now, I would advise you to close your eyes and go deeper into hypnosis, and let your 'hypnotic mind' have reign for a minute. I need to talk to it, and not your critical mind. You'll get why in a while, so please, again, suspend your disbelief, and your judgment, and let yourself be freed to take an unconscious journey with me.

Great! Glad you're on board!

I want you to think about why the 'critical faculty' rejects ideas that don't make sense straightaway.

Let's go back to children. They're developing. They're forming beliefs. They're being conditioned. Yet, they're not as conditioned as us adults, who are conditioned to see the world in a particular light, and to reject what we don't believe, and to accept what we do. Children are impressionable, right? Children are naïve, are they not? It is us adults who have it right! We are the ones who've learnt the lessons that are important. We're the ones all on the same page, am I right? We are the logical ones. We rationalize. We 'critically think' for goodness sake! Children, heck, they believe in fairytales, and goblins, and ghosts and fantasy lands and make believe, and, well, yes, I've already said it, but—pretend!

When I was a child, growing up, I had this really magical mother. She used to play make believe and pretend with my brother and sister and I.

Once upon a time, when I was quite young, my mother tendered us children to NEVER FORGET something. She said, and, please take not I have never forgotten her words:

> *"Never stop believing in make believe or playing pretend; children, it's the only thing that's real in this world!"*

I want to explore why our 'critical faculty' allows some things in and some things not to enter our minds. This is taken from the field of neuro-linguistic programming (NLP).

In NLP there is a presupposition that goes: Everybody lives in their own model of the world. A presupposition, by the way, is something we take as a 'given'; that is, something we accept and undertake to be true.

This NLP presupposition assumes that everybody is different in their unique understanding of the world, their beliefs, the way they perceive the world to be, and so on. Why is this though? Why might your persuasions be different than other peoples?

NLP teaches that the 'critical faculty' is a metaphorical structure comprised of five things; namely: (a) beliefs, (b) values, (c) memories, (d) thinking pattens, and (e) state. What exactly are all these you ask? No problem:

- Beliefs: A belief is something believed to be true, whether it is or not.

- Values: A value is something we regard as important.

- Memories: A memory is a recollection of an experience from the past.

- Thinking Patterns: Thinking patterns are the way in which we think.

- State: A state is how we feel at the present moment (e.g., sad, happy, etc.)

Beliefs, Values, Memories, Thinking Patterns, and our present State of mind are the psychological factors that have us rule an idea out or reel it in; that is, accept or reject. Everybody has differences in these areas. Nobody is the same. This is the presupposition of NLP and why you can assume it to be true. All you have to do is ask honestly yourself: "Do I know, or have I met, anyone, ever, who has shared exactly the same beliefs, values, memories, thinking patterns, or present state of mind as me?" My answer is a resounding "No!" How about your answer?

So how does this work, exactly? What are the drivers behind why we might accept something into our mind or reject it outright? The answer lies in how we all have different 'intensities' about each of these categorical factors, regarding their level of importance—for example, you may believe you're going to lose your job tomorrow based on your current state as well as your thinking patterns. This belief may be believed to be true, but may change after tomorrow has passed and you find you still have your job. Or, you may believe you need a new car, but you believe that your current car still has some life in it, and thus you may not go out immediately and purchase a new car; yet, you might. You see it all depends on your thinking patterns, your state (e.g., Are you excited or stressed about thinking about having to buy a new car?). Excitement is a buying state, whereas stress is a state in which most people refrain from taking a buying action.

Really get this, because if you can evidently see someone is stressed you'll know from knowing this that they probably are not going to go out and buy a new car tomorrow. However, if you evidently see they're excite and a new car is all they can talk about, and as they do you see their face light up like a child fantasizing about Santa coming, then you can likelier than not predict accurately that they'll be driving home in a new car soon; rather than later.

So if persuasion is your game, and you want to change minds and influence people to take an action you want them to take all of this can surely be helpful for you to know. By understanding why people reject information out right or accept it with a great big hug of love and acceptance only takes analyzing a person from the vantage of these five criteria. You simply need to know their beliefs, know their values, know some about their past, understand how they think, and be aware of their current state of mind. It really is that simple.

Knowing all of this you can form your stories around these five critical considerations. So if someone is experiencing a 'bad' mood, one that you predict is not going to get you the keys to their car so you can take your date to the movies later that evening, maybe, and I'm only making a suggestion here, but, maybe you might want to tell a story that shifts them from being in a 'bad' mood to a 'good' mood, and then ask them for their keys. Just a thought! Just a thought!

If the same person has a belief that lending their car to anyone is a mistake, you might want to share a story about someone who was entrusted with someone's care and brought it back unscratched, with a hundred dollar bill in the console. Just a thought. Just a thought.

The 'Hypnotic Mind' Makes Its Own Meanings

Also keep in mind that if you're telling a hypnotic story you can tell any ambiguous story, using hypnotic intonation, which can be even a simple story; yet, the 'hypnotic mind' will make its own meanings from—meanings that won't likely make any logical sense to you whatsoever.

The 'hypnotic mind' is a metaphoric mind, and makes meanings from associations that it makes through subliminal references.

A train is coming at you, and you don't know why, and yet, you still sense something is coming up from somewhere mysterious, which will likely change the course of your life forever. This short metaphoric story is not intentionally meant to have any meaning whatsoever. I can assure you, however, that it has all sorts of 'hypnotic' meanings that will be interpreted by your subject's unconscious mind.

I'm sharing this point with you, because it's important to realize there will be times when you don't think you're penetrating your subject's 'hypnotic mind' –and, it may even be that you are told by the person telling you the story that your story is meaningless to you in some matter of speaking candidly. Don't believe them and believe what they're conveying to you is necessarily the 'truth', because I'm telling you from experience that I've told people these same types of stories, got the stares, and sure enough the embedded suggestions I planted in those stories were acted upon and I got the outcome I was hoping for. You have to trust that when you're hypnotic storytelling that your stories are working in ways mysterious to your own conscious understanding.

NLP Perceptual Positions

In NLP there are three perceptual positions. You need to know these as different from what writers refer to as the 'perspectives' and I'll tell you why here shortly.

A perceptual position is our own observation from a particular point of view. Here are the three NLP perceptual positions defined:

- First Perceptual Position: Observing things from our own personal perspective; namely, how we, ourselves, perceive an interaction, experience, or object, etc.

- Second Perceptual Position: Observing someone else's thoughts, feelings, and model of the world, by mentally stepping out of our shoes and into their shoes. When we do, we see the world from how they might likely perceive it. We assume their beliefs, their values, their memories, their thinking patterns, and their current state. We imaginatively become them mentally.

- Third Perceptual Position: Observing from a detached bystander's perspective the interaction taking place between our self and the second person; namely, stepping into this non-attached person's shoes to observe the interaction or experience occurring. When we do we do this we imagine what their perception is regarding the interchange of communication between ourselves and the other person.

These perceptual positions allow us to consider many things: (a) what the character's in our hypnotic stories are like, (b) how our hypnotic subject will likely perceive our hypnotic story, or even us, and (c) they allow us to consider from a third person's perception how we are performing as a hypnotic storyteller, and how hypnotized, or not, is our hypnotic subject. You want to have a well-rounded perception of your interactions and how you communicate your stores to others. You don't want to only rely on your own beliefs, values, memories, thought patterns, and the state you're in. You want to also be able to observe other people's beliefs, values, memories, thought patterns, and the current state they're in. Doing so will help you mindfully develop and achieve the well-formed outcomes you desire.

NLP Metaphors

NLP metaphors is a quick storytelling technique that, in my opinion, parallels must of the 'type' of work that Milton Erickson did when telling stories.

These types of hypnotic stories require you to first take an understanding of the NLP model of behavior. I've already taught that life experiences from childhood onward throughout adulthood creates beliefs, values, memories, thinking patterns, as well as states of mind we identify with at any given moment in time. The behavior model stems off from this in which decisions are filtered through the 'critical faculty'; namely: (a) beliefs, (b) values, (c) memories, (d) thinking patterns, and (e) the state you're in now, which influences a decision to be made. In other words, do we act positively towards the suggestion, neutrally, negatively, or outright reject what we're suggested? This influence governed by the critical faculty matrix causes the choices we make. Once a choice has been decided the behavior becomes the actions we take.

We can actually reverse engineer this model as well. When we do we learn what an individual's beliefs, values, memories, thinking patterns, and what is the current state of mind they're in.

How do we do this you ask? Simple! First we work backward in reverse to observe our subject's recent behavior. This gives us the information to observe the recent actions they've taken. Then from knowing their actions, we discover what recent choices they've made which would have led to said action being taken. When we know what choices they've made we can probe through asking questions what their state of mind was at the time they made the decision, what was going through their mind at the time (i.e., thinking patterns), and possibly from this learn more about their beliefs that governed their decision, as well as get insights into what was important to them (i.e., values), and likely learn some about their past (i.e., memories).

After gaining this valuable information we've in a sense gained entry into their model of reality. We can thus begin to utilize Second Perceptual Position to get inside this model of reality—to become them mentally for the purpose of modeling them.

Now, after arriving at this understanding of them, you're in a position to finally take a problem they have and create an NLP metaphor which simply means you'll quickly devise a short story which mirrors their problem, spinning it in such a way that your subject's 'hypnotic mind' will indirectly create the meanings from your hypnotic story to change future behaviors or to take certain actions.

Reverse engineering to discover the psychological pro-file of the individual subject is a great way also for influ-encing and persuading them to do what you want. You can hypnotically change minds; yet, also develop NLP metaphors to change to instil inside their 'hypnotic mind' indirect hypnotic messages that will alter their experi-ences mentally, which in turn will alter their beliefs, val-ues, memories, thought patterns, and put them into a new more resourceful state of mind—all by way of hypnotic storytelling.

The Recap

In this chapter on NLP and hypnotic storytelling you learnt the reason why children are so adept at hypnotic storytelling. You learnt how many of our life experiences have restricted our hypnotic storytelling faculties. These experiences lead us to form rigidity in our belief systems, regardless if our beliefs are true or not. These life experi-ences instil in us values that we perceive as important as-pects to consider in the decision making process. These life experiences also have us form memories which teach us valuable lessons; namely, what is useful or useless, help-ful or hurtful, empowering or disempowering. These memories are the acid tests we use to disambiguate un-sureness and disorientation we may experience when faced with making a future decision in order to avoid what we don't want (pain), while moving more nearer to what we do want (pleasure). We make a lot of decisions based on our past experiences which we revisit through our memories. These life experiences also create our thought patterns, which we use to sort information mentally before making a decision to act on something new or not. In many ways, our current state is determined by experiences and the emotions associated or anchored to those experiences. This is one reason why someone who has had a past experience of being sold something under pressure only to later experience cognitive dissonance, i.e. 'buyers-remorse', may, when the hypnotic subject feels this way again, in the future, might refrain from making another purchase. Certain states come to us by our physiology, energy levels, and the emotions others near or around us are likewise experiencing. States are contagious so when one person is feeling down-in-the-dumps depressed, those in their company may find themselves feeling depressed as well.

In this chapter you also learnt that the 'hypnotic mind' makes its own meanings from hypnotic stories which the subject's conscious critical mind will likely not understand. This is similar to when we have a fragmented dream in which we remember that seems to make no sense whatsoever may quite well make sense to us logically at some point in the future—the light bulb in our 'mind' goes off and 'gets-it'. The hypnotic mind is always processing and construing higher meaning from all the information slipping into it; however, it usually takes the conscious critical mind some time to catch up and critically make sense of this coded information. Once the 'hypnotic minds' code has been cracked the conscious mind can construct linguistically the meaning which will then make sense to other people we communicate with intellectually.

In this chapter you also learnt about NLP perceptual positions which can be a brilliant method of getting hypnotically inside your subject's model of reality, as well as perceive interactions from a third person perception, as well. Using these perceptual positions we get clarity into the beliefs, values, thinking patterns, past, and current state of mind of our subjects. In this way we learn their motivations and persuasions in order to effectively help them change beliefs, values, thought patterns, new perceptions about their past, and in turn more positive states of mind in the present circumstance. Understanding perceptual positions and your subject's model of the world through NLP perceptual positions also helps you discover how your subject codes and evaluates information presented in in certain ways. By getting a sense of their tendencies we can forecast with greater probabilities what our subject's will likely do when confronted with a specific new choice. This is useful for changing minds and shaping new behaviors and beliefs in our subject.

Lastly, I covered and you learnt how to put all these NLP learnings into sync with one another to tell NLP metaphors, which you learnt were parallel stories that gave a different unconscious perspective that would get hypnotically processed in the 'hypnotic mind' to afterward, later on, bring about positive changes in our subjects, by shifting their beliefs, values, hypnotic thought patterns, previous memories, and in return their state of mind, opening the subject up to perceiving experiences differently to in turn help them to make better decisions, which in turn would lead the hypnotic subject to take better actions that would lead to an overall more desired outcome.

Once you're able to get inside the mind of your hypnotic subject it becomes more probabilistic that you'll effectively be able to manipulate, persuade, influence, and change their minds, attitudes, feelings, decisions, and, yes, even their actions/behaviors. It really is this easy—all through sharing a simply; yet, relative, NLP metaphor that might make no sense to them consciously, but hypnotically make perfect sense to their 'hypnotic mind'.

The Next Step

Academically, I can tell you the step-by-step logic of the psychological principles applied to NLP and hypnotic storytelling; namely, as it relates to understanding the critical faculty and the matrix of beliefs, values, thought patterns, memories, and states of mind, and also delivering of NLP metaphors. However, I know it wouldn't make you a better hypnotic storyteller or neuro-linguist, just more knowledgeable on these subjects.

As I've mentioned I believe that learning comes by doing, and testing for yourself the lessons in this book. I think all learning first happens at the unconscious hypnotic level, and that the conscious mind requires more time to catch up to what you already have learnt unconsciously or hypnotically, already.

With hypnotic storytelling you have already inside you the knowledge and learnings to be able to capably well tell

hypnotizing stories. In truth, you already tell hypnotic stories without even being aware when you do.

This book walks you through the process of hypnotic
storytelling in a unique way that brings with it even more
clarity than what you're used to. It is better not to
overthink NLP and Hypnotic Storytelling, the Zeirgarnik
Effect, Nested Loop Sequences, and Hypnotic Language,
because as soon as you do, you stop being quite so hypnotic in your deliver. The more rigid your learning by way
of overthinking complex hypnotic storytelling and NLP
models, the less freedom you have to express yourself hypnotically. The key, then, now, is to do hypnotic storytelling hypnotically, while learning this information through
the indirect hypnotic learning approach I'm covertly delivering to you in this book.

These exercises will help prepare you to tell hypnotic
stories without your critical thinking getting in the way.
The 'hypnotic mind' is the 'other mind' which has already
learnt the Hypnotic Hero's Journey Model, the Hypnotic
Language Predicates that linguistically and affectively
construct hypnotic realities from the hypnotic stories you
tell using them, that I've presented to you, even the
Zeirgarnik Effect, Hypnotic Nested Loop Sequences, and
Hypnotic Fractionation that can be implemented into
your hypnotic stories, the tenets of Hypnotic Language,
and now NLP and Hypnotic Storytelling using perceptual
positions and highly hypnotic NLP metaphors. I ask you
to suspend your disbelief and trust in the process, and let
your stories hypnotize your subjects hypnotically. Play
with using the hypnotic language patterns I've given you

to study, as well as the Milton Model and Meta Model to be able to discover in your own mind experientially where your mind travels, and how your subject's react as you layer hypnotic language into your hypnotic stories, as well as the newest NLP behavior model, perceptual positions model, and the hypnotic NLP metaphor making model. Consider this blind faith in your 'hypnotic mind' comparable to riding a bicycle you've already learnt to ride. You might at any moment mount a bicycle in the future and ride it without your conscious mind's interference—astonishingly! In the same way, think about now using NLP metaphors to do the same and position yourself as an amazingly hypnotic, hypnotizing storyteller that can put your subject's under the spell of hypnosis just like that.

Have a think about that as you become taken aback by your 'hypnotic mind's' ability to affect real change in others—gaining you everything in life you want.

CHAPTER 7

THE HOLISTIC HYPNOSIS MODEL

I appreciate you taking the time to read this book and do the exercises which have followed each chapter thus far. This is the last chapter, but I've saved the best for last.

When I was a young child my mother was a prominent hypnotherapist—one of the best I've personally ever known. I was indoctrinated into hypnosis from an early age, and followed, I guess you might say, in my mother's footsteps.

I am an expert in hypnosis; that is, as a trainer, but also as a practitioner. What I'm going to share with you in this final chapter is the greatest hypnosis insight I may have ever received. I've held it a secret until now.

This secret is The Holistic Hypnosis Model. Let me share it with you as you go into a deep hypnotic trance now.

The greatest secret I've ever learnt regarding hypnosis came by way of applying hypnosis to myself one night, before bed. While hypnotized I discovered a hypnosis secret so profound that it changed the way I hypnotized people altogether.

I want you to think about Milton Hyland Erickson. In my opinion he's one of the best hypnotists who's ever lived. I'll tell you why.

Erickson was known for the utilization principle. This principle insight I discovered, in my opinion, goes deeper in some respects than what even Erickson himself would come to know. The utilization principle states that the hypnotist use whatever is in the subject's awareness to hypnotize the subject.

Erickson used this approach in what's been coined the Non-Awareness Set. Instead of using objects or aspects of what your hypnotic subjects tells you to hypnotize them; the non-awareness set utilizes instead the naturally occurring unconscious movements and responses of your hypnotic subject—for example, a crossing of the arms or legs, or the unconscious positioning of the hypnotic subject in the hypnosis chair, or even something as diminutive as an unconscious arm movement or knee jerk reaction.

Imagine me sitting face-to-face with you telling you that because your leg just flinched unconsciously it means you're going into a deep 'sleepy' hypnotic trance and you haven't yet realized it yet, but it's happening just as unconsciously as that knee jerk. Imagine me adding that when you do realize you're going into a deep state of hypnosis that it will be too late for you to do anything about it, because you'll already be so hypnotized that you find it impossible to keep your eyes open. Don't close them, yet. We have this last chapter of the book to get through, and then, only after you're finished with this chapter, will you allow your hypnotic mind to process all of these learnings that you've learnt in such a way that your conscious mind will start getting profound hypnotic insights automatically, randomly, and more and more frequent as time passes.

Erickson's utilization approach is brilliant, I thought, when I first learnt of it and used it. In fact, I've never had it fail to hypnotize a subject and put them deep under hypnosis.

I needed to tell you about this utilization approach because it is from this approach that my holistic hypnosis model was born in the hypnotic 'homa-fire' of my mind.

You see the greatest secret to hypnosis is that everything is hypnotic. Everything.

As a formally trained hypnotist I both learnt theories and models, yet also practiced hypnosis applicably and regularly. Referent power came to me as a result by other hypnotists and sales professionals who observed me applying these principles and applications to my sales calls. What I learnt from my insight is that everything is hypnotic; meaning, everything causes hypnosis or has the potential to cause hypnosis.

This is why the utilization approach worked so well for Erickson himself. Everything he utilized caused hypnosis to happen in the subject.

The Holistic Model takes into account everything; namely, for example, both direct and indirect communication models, implicit and explicit approaches, any belief, any thought, any movement, anything.

This Holistic Model approach to hypnosis only requires you to use hypnosis to hypnotize someone else—that's it—end of story!

Think about how empowering this is for you; especially, as it relates back to your hypnotic storytelling abilities. You can hypnotize anyone with any story you tell so long as it is your desire to hypnotize your subject. You can hypnotize anyone. Think about how empowered this makes you feel. Think about how much confidence you can have knowing you don't even have to think about hypnotizing someone; yet, they will still fall under your hypnotic spell!

The easiest way I can prove this to you is to have you take notice of the fact that you're hypnotized right now. That's it. Really consider to what extent you're hypnotized, as you may be more hypnotized that you think you are. Pretty good proof, aye?

When this profound insight came to me that pretty astonishing night, I had to test it. So I went to bed early, and as soon as I woke up I visited my sister and looked at her in a way that got her attention. She said to me: "What's wrong?" And that's when I said, "Brandi, my eyes don't deceive me, you're hypnotized. I know, because I know the difference between not getting enough sleep and someone who is hypnotized. You're hypnotized, aren't you? How does it feel being hypnotized, sis?"

She paused. She contemplated my analysis of her state. Then she said, "I feel a bit spacy I suppose. But I feel really good, Bryan."

I said back, "I know what you mean; it feels fantastic when you're hypnotized. I love how it makes me feel. It's like, you're in a whole different world, one that's not temporal, but forever feeling."

My sister started going even deeper into hypnosis. Her non-verbal language was giving away all the clues. I didn't have to do any special induction, or snap my fingers, or anything, except besides to tell her the *Your Hypnotized* story, as I've just explained. It's a great feeling to float in your mind. You do it all the time when you're not consciously paying attention.

You are aware of everything; yet, not aware.

The Hypnotic Storyteller's Indirect Approach

So my sister was the first person I hypnotized without trying to hypnotize her; explicitly, relying only on my own hypnotic state to hypnotize her. But you ask, "What about a more covert approach? How would you have hypnotized your sister had you not wanted to point out that she was hypnotized, directly?"

That's a great question, and indirectly I've already given you the answer. Don't be so confused. Let me explain.

The story I told you about my sister becoming hypnotized was a covert hypnotic story I told you. It got your attention, it caused a trans-derivational search to happen in your mind which caused you to think about my sister becoming instantly hypnotized, which in turn caused you to mentally imagine what that was like, and likewise instantly become hypnotized. My humble apologies—you were already hypnotized—I forgot.

Anyhow, this is the indirect approach for applying the Holistic Hypnosis Model. You can tell a story about anybody you want taking on some altered hypnotic state; such as, appearing as though they were on drugs, hadn't slept in a month, had ate one too many carbohydrates and not enough proteins, or simply that this character in your story looked hypnotized or mesmerized having a blank zombie like expression on their face. When you do, you'll begin seeing the signs of hypnosis happening immediately. It's so powerful, so easy, so enthralling to think about; yet, in any case, it works all the same. Everything is hypnotic. So long as you're mildly hypnotized you can hypnotize anybody else without any effort whatsoever. This is because the 'hypnotic mind' is affected by hypnosis. Hypnosis, the condition, is instantly contagious, and people become quickly infected by being around other people who happen to be hypnotized. It is an affective state that causes others to be affected hypnotically as well. The more hypnotized you are, the more hypnotized others around you become—they can't help it.

Ericksonian Psychotherapy and Positive Expectancy Techniques Applied to Hypnotic Storytelling Frameworks

Erickson had five different means by which he created 'positive expectancy' in his psychotherapy clients; namely: (a) congruency, (b) positive framing, (c) implication of success, (d) defining and expanding expectations, and (e) building self-image.

Positive expectancy is an attitude the hypnotists must have, and in context of psychotherapy it is important to maintain. Congruence is one method Erickson utilized. Simply stated, congruence is an indirect and permissive, non-authoritarian approach that maintains that what you expect to happen your hypnotic subject will likewise expect to happen as well. Congruence runs over from mere words into non-verbal communication as well. In order to operate congruently that your hypnotic subject will believe what you believe, it is important to believe what you want them to believe and this be reflected in your voice, body movements, and all unconscious behavior as well. Everything should reflect this positive expectation, else your subjects may not believe your belief in them is true.

When you frame your persuasions you should likewise do so adopting a 'positive frame'. This means adhering to the NLP presupposition that all behavior is an attempt to solve a problem, or accomplish a goal. Erickson referred to positive framing of problem behavior as the 'apposition of opposites'. This is simply praising how well someone does an unwanted behavior to hypnotically suggest that they are able to do something so well. In effect, this approach will force them to more seek out the solution, even on the unconscious level.

Next you want to imply success in your hypnotic storytelling. This means future pacing the subject's problem as being solved in order to have the subject indirectly stimulate their own thinking and become transported into a resourceful mindset that is advantageous for problem solving.

When you define and expand on the expectations you have for your hypnotic subject you help create hypnotic self-fulfilling prophecies that will 'haunt' the subject until the desired outcome is reached. Erickson quoted saying once: "You can pretend anything and master it." By having your hypnotic subjects expand their beliefs from impossibilities into believed possibilities the come to expect they can achieve their goals; that is to say, this creates positive expectancy, too.

In many psychotherapies that utilize hypnosis the building of self-image is used to create greater expectancy that in the future some desired result will be achieved. In AA and NA programs one way this is accomplished is by having the subject concentrate on today's behaviors and being okay with them, even though other people may disagree with the behavior. In doing this, self-acceptance is achieved, as well as the positive expectancy that 'someday' I'll meet my goal.

The reason I mention these Ericksonian psychotherapy approaches is to have you firsthand conceive how positive expectancy; especially, though maintaining congruency will work in other contexts as well to stimulate rapid hypnosis. Congruity is mesmeric and will mirror back to you what you mirror to your hypnotic subjects.

When you're telling a hypnotic story your expectation of expectancy must be the expectation that your hypnotic subject will be hypnotized. You must reflect this with your hypnotic unconscious mannerisms, as well as your conscious thought patterns, your physiology, your hypnotic language patterns, and of course you want to have only 'positive' expectations as your hypnotic thought patterns.

The Recap

Hypnosis happens irrespective of any formal inductions, techniques, models, or theories. The best way to become a master hypnotic storyteller is to apply these lessons in this book, while also making practice, practice, practice your hypnotic mantra. The real education in hypnosis comes when you do a little self-hypnosis to enter a mild hypnotic trance and then with positive expectancy, compliance, and congruence hypnotize person after person until you feel competent, confident, and start to hypnotize people unconsciously without thinking about it.

Let me share one last final hypnotic story.

This morning, I was extremely hypnotized, and Jennifer asked me to go to a nearby fast-food restaurant and get us some breakfast.

I went to order, and very quickly started to notice the cashier dropping into hypnosis. Like I say, I was extremely hypnotized myself.

When the cashier attempted to read back my order she kept saying I ordered egg on my breakfast sandwich instead of cheese. I told her once more it was cheese I wanted and not egg. She said, "That's what I said!" I then asked her to please read it back again. Once again she mentioned 'egg' instead of 'cheese'; which was not what I ordered.

Finally, knowing she was deeply hypnotized, I explained to her how she was hypnotized and how it was my fault. I explained to her how I am much of my day hypnotized, as I am always hypnotized when I'm writing, or doing some work project. I tend to operate better and I fully trust my 'hypnotic mind' to do a brilliant job without my conscious mind hampering progress.

Anyhow I explained this to her and she looked at me knowing how truthful I was being with her. She sensed my sincerity and positive expectancy and of course I was completely congruent and not authoritarian or harshly direct with her. I told her to please check to see if the sandwiches had cheese or egg on them and she said, "Oh. Okay. I see now. Yes. I did put you down for 'cheese' and not egg. I kept saying 'egg' didn't I?"

I told her it was not problem and that it's not her fault but rather mine. The manager eventually came over and brought my food. The cashier who'd waited on me told her I'd hypnotized her. I smiled, and before I could leave the manager asked, "Can you hypnotize me?"

I stared at her with my hypnotic gaze and then about 30 seconds later and told her 'now' you're hypnotized, aren't you? And because you're hypnotized you can work without thinking about it the rest of the day, can you not?

Because you do know how to do that don't you?" Each time I asked a question she shook her head compliantly and eventually I gave her the suggestion that she may want to keep an eye on orders coming through the drive-thru. She complied completely and zombie walked back to the back of the restaurant to check on the drive-thru.

The woman at the register said, "My God, you're good!"

My final bit on this is to advise: that to the extent you try hard to master these learnings in hypnotic storytelling you'll limit yourself more. To the extent you tell your hypnotic stories by letting your 'hypnotic mind' do all the work, you'll be a fantastic hypnotic storyteller.

The Next Step

Finally we reach the end. Hypnotic Storytelling is a powerfully indirect and covert method for conversationally hypnotizing your unsuspecting subjects. Things to keep in mind are: (a) you can hypnotize anyone with or without trying to hypnotize them, (b) it is important to know how to read trance-signs to know when someone is hypnotized or not, (c) the easiest and quickest way to hypnotize someone is to hypnotize yourself first and have inside you, but also create inside them too 'positive expectancy', (d) experiences create beliefs, values, memories, thought patterns, and your current state.

Experiences, I've mentioned are the catalyst for why we're all different, all experiencing reality through the prism of different models, and are attributable to the naturally occurring phenomenon known as hypnosis. Reality really is plastic, and not as real as most people imagine, but what is real is nothing, and as confusing as this may sound, or be difficult to comprehend, it is the true reality I believe. We are always hypnotized to some degree. It is our critical thinking and overthinking which get in the way of the hypnotic state. As you grow as a hypnotic storyteller you'll discover how it is possible to consciously be hypnotized and operate on a meta-level. This is how I live my life, day to day, having been a hypnotist since childhood. The more hypnotic stories you tell the more hypnotic you'll become. You'll be astonished when you find that everyone around you cannot help but slip into hypnosis. This happens to most everyone I come into contact with on a daily basis.

I've sat through job interviews and watched those interviewing me drop under the spell of hypnosis—I was always given the job. I've sat through sales calls where I sold yellow-pages advertising to small and medium size businesses and telling these hypnotic stories, hypnotized myself, watched my potential customers become instant customers—always making it to number one with whatever company I decided to partner with. I've taught countless workshops and seminars on hypnosis/NLP and never get bored watching hypnotists being hypnotized, or the amazing psychotherapeutic change work that goes on to change lives at such events.

I now present you with the last exercises that will make you completely confident with your ability to hypnotize others by telling a simple hypnotic story. After you complete these exercises you will deserve a pat on the back, because you'll be well on your way to becoming a 'master' hypnotic storyteller.

I.   Hypnotize yourself and then engage someone who is not hypnotized and tell them a hypnotic story. It doesn't have to be real long, and in fact can be only a few lines that you tell. Record mentally what happens to the subject; namely, observe the trance-signs that happen.

II. Make a small portfolio of hypnotic stories and be sure to add in embedded commands, hypnotic language patterns, character development using the NLP perceptual positions and decision making model, and all of the other concepts covered throughout this book. This portfolio only has to consist of 10 – 20 hypnotic stories. Know them well and practice telling them as often as you can. You see Milton Erickson himself used to tell many of the same stories over and over again, because he knew they worked.

III. Listen to a hypnotic download each night before you go to bed. These can be picked up for less than $10 at www.indirectknowledge.com. As you listen to them regularly you'll be amazed at how well you begin speaking hypnotically because of the hidden hypnotic language patterns in the downloads. The more you listen

the more hypnotic you'll conversationally become, and the more spellbinding your stories
will be.

BIBLIOGRAPHY

Campbell, J. (2004). *The hero with a thousand faces* (Commemorative ed.). Princeton, NJ: Princeton University Press.

Hill, B. (2011). *Coach yourself to writing success: Boost motivation, increase creativity and achieve your writing goals: Teach Yourself.* Chicago: McGraw-Hill Co.

Hill, B. (2013). *NLP for writers.* Great Britain: Hodder & Stoughton.

Kavaler, R. (1986). *Tigers in the wood.* Urbana: University of Illinois Press.

Ledochowski, I. (2001). *The power of conversational hypnosis.* Washington: Street Hypnosis.

Ledochowski, I. (2003). *The deep trance training manual.* Carmarthen, Wales ; Williston, VT: Crown House Pub.

Murphy, J. (1963). *The power of your subconscious mind.* Englewood Cliffs, N.J.: Prentice-Hall.

Murphy, J. (2002). *Think yourself to health, wealth amp; Happiness: The best of Joseph Murphy's cosmic wisdom.* New York: Reward.

Watts, N. (2006). *Writing a novel: Teach yourself.* Chicago: McGraw-Hill.

Westra, B. (2010). *Language patterns* (p. 2). Thonotosassa: Indirect Knowledge Limited.

Westra, B. (2012). *Indirect knowledge.* Retrieved from http://www.indirectknowledge.com

Westra, B. (2012). *Indirect knowledge: Lessons in covert indirect hypnosis and much more from the popular blog:*

Www.indirectknowledge.com. Murray, KY: Indirect Knowledge Limited.

Westra, B. (2013). *NLP and hypnosis: Influence and persuasions patterns.* Murray, KY: Indirect Knowledge Limited.

Westra, B. (2014). *A manual for creating conversational hypnotists* (pp. 33-95). Murray, KY: Indirect Knowledge Limited.

Zeig, J. K. (Ed.). (1994). *Ericksonian methods: The essence of the story.* New York, NY: Brunner/Mazel.

Zeigarnik, B. (1938). *On finished and unfinished tasks* (pp. 300-314). A source book of Gestalt psychology.

INDEX

clarity, 45, 51, 88, 111, 118, 119, 137, 145, 148, 167, 171, 184, 186
cognitively, 87, 171
come, 132, 149, 154
communicate, 40, 71, 78, 84, 117, 118, 120, 122, 128, 135, 138, 140, 165, 169, 179, 184
communicating, 11, 17, 54, 71, 89, 92, 117, 118, 127, 153
comparative deletion patterns, 131
complex equivalence patterns, 125
conceptualize, 86
confused, 131, 138
consciously, 120, 121, 160
construct, 138
constructions, 85, 86, 169
conversational hypnosis, 84, 119, 128, 129, 130, 134, 141, 164, 166, 205
conversational postulate patterns, 131
cookie-cutter templates, 74

covert, 17, 87, 93, 98, 100, 101, 193, 199, 205
covertly, 118, 147, 164
critical faculty, 14, 27, 43, 44, 56, 58, 73, 83, 100, 136, 172, 173, 174, 180, 185
critical mind, 119, 139
defocus, 72
deletion, 131, 142
different, 117, 124, 136, 137, 138, 154, 159
direct, 133, 155
dissociation, 154
dissonance, 129, 148
double bind, 128, 129
embedded, 161, 162
embedded command, 161, 162
emotions, 156, 159
Erickson, 11, 12, 14, 15, 142, 190, 191, 195, 196
evaded, 164
everyday, 116
everything, 126, 128, 136
experiencing, 11, 12, 35, 39, 41, 58, 99, 101, 102, 125, 160, 176, 183, 199
explicit, 83, 116, 145, 192

FINAL THOUGHTS FROM THE AUTHOR

My whole life I've been hypnotized; when I weren't, I'd wish I were. This is another book I present you with: one about Hypnotic Storytelling. Stories are a powerful vehicle for hypnotizing others. I hope you enjoy this book, and will read others of mine, which you can find at:

www.indirectknowledge.com

Learn Well; Live Well!
Bryan James Westra

www.ingramcontent.com/pod-product-compliance
Lightning Source LLC
Chambersburg PA
CBHW020609270326
41927CB00005B/255